Manifest Destiny and the Coming of the Civil War

1840–1861

GOLDENTREE BIBLIOGRAPHIES

In American History
under the series editorship of
Arthur S. Link

Manifest Destiny and the Coming of the Civil War

1840–1861

compiled by

Don E. Fehrenbacher

Stanford University

APPLETON-CENTURY-CROFTS

Educational Division

New York   MEREDITH CORPORATION

Editor's Foreword

GOLDENTREE BIBLIOGRAPHIES IN AMERICAN HISTORY are designed to provide students, teachers, and librarians with ready and reliable guides to the literature of American history in all its remarkable scope and variety. Volumes in the series cover comprehensively the major periods in American history, while additional volumes are devoted to all important subjects.

Goldentree Bibliographies attempt to steer a middle course between the brief list of references provided in the average textbook and the long bibliography in which significant items are often lost in the sheer number of titles listed. Each bibliography is, therefore, selective, with the sole criterion for choice being the significance—and not the age—of any particular work. The result is bibliographies of all works, including journal articles and doctoral dissertations, that are still useful, without bias in favor of any particular historiographical school.

Each compiler is a scholar long associated, both in research and teaching, with the period or subject of his volume. All compilers have not only striven to accomplish the objective of this series but have also cheerfully adhered to a general style and format. However, each compiler has been free to define his field, make his own selections, and work out internal organization as the unique demands of his period or subject have seemed to dictate.

The single great objective of *Goldentree Bibliographies in American History* will have been achieved if these volumes help researchers and students to find their way to the significant literature of American history.

Arthur S. Link

v

Preface

Although it stresses westward expansion and the sectional controversy, this bibliography comprehends the general history of the United States from 1840 to 1861. The listing is necessarily selective, especially so in the case of primary sources, but for students and teachers there may be considerable usefulness in a work that occupies middle ground between the exhaustive professional bibliography and the brief reference lists found in the average textbook. The bibliography includes only published material and dissertations available on microfilm. With a few exceptions, it omits public documents, such as legislative journals, and works that are primarily nonhistorical, such as studies in economic theory and literary criticism. Some subjects herein given limited attention are more extensively covered, or soon will be, in other *Goldentree Bibliographies*.

It must be emphasized that the chapters and subdivisions of this bibliography are organizational conveniences and often do not include all the works relevant to their respective headings. The general works in Chapter I are not listed again in later chapters. Titles under the subheading "General Studies" are not listed again in the same chapter. Bibliographical and historiographical works, as well as source materials, are grouped together in each chapter and are not listed again under other subheadings in that chapter. Thus, someone looking for writings on "Slavery" will naturally turn first to the section so titled in Chapter VII; but he will also find relevant and important materials in other sections of that chapter, in sections on "The Negro" and "Religion" in Chapter V, and in the "General Studies" section of Chapter I. Only by greatly increasing the number of cross-references, and thereby greatly reducing the total number of titles, could the compiler have made each subdivision a complete little bibliography in itself. Instead, he elected to settle for something less than maximum accessibility in order to achieve maximum coverage within the prescribed limitations of space. Many cross-references are in fact, provided, and these, together with the table of contents and the index of authors, should enable the user of this bibliography to find what he wants with little trouble.

Unless otherwise noted, entries are arranged alphabetically by author. The date given with the title of a book is, as a rule, the year of original publication. A dagger (†) indicates that a paperback edition of the book was listed as in print when this bibliography went to press. The index and cross-reference numerals direct the reader to page and position-on-the-page. Thus, "42.17" indicates the seventeenth entry on page 42. Extra-wide margins provide space for writing in library call numbers. Extra space at the bottom of many pages permits handwritten additions to the listing.

Don E. Fehrenbacher

Abbreviations

Ag Hist	*Agricultural History*
Ala Rev	*Alabama Review*
Am Hist Rev	*American Historical Review*
Am Lit	*American Literature*
Am Pol Sci Rev	*American Political Science Review*
Am Q	*American Quarterly*
Am Schol	*American Scholar*
Ann Iowa	*Annals of Iowa*
Ann Rep Am Hist Assn	*Annual Report, American Historical Association*
Ariz W	*Arizona and the West*
Ark Hist Q	*Arkansas Historical Quarterly*
Bus Hist Rev	*Business History Review*
Calif Hist Soc Q	*California Historical Society Quarterly*
Car Inst Pub	*Carnegie Institute Publications*
Chi Hist	*Chicago History*
Civ War Hist	*Civil War History*
Colo Mag	*Colorado Magazine*
Contrib Ed (Peabody)	*George Peabody College Contributions to Education*
Econ Pol Sci Ser (Wis)	*Economics and Political Science Series*, University of Wisconsin
Fla Hist Q	*Florida Historical Quarterly*
Ga Hist Q	*Georgia Historical Quarterly*
Har Law Rev	*Harvard Law Review*
Hist Ed Q	*History of Education' Quarterly*
Hist Soc S Calif Q	*Historical Society of Southern California Quarterly*
Hist Theory	*History and Theory*
Hist Today	*History Today*
Hunt Lib Bull	*Huntington Library Bulletin*
Hunt Lib Q	*Huntington Library Quarterly*
Ind Mag Hist	*Indiana Magazine of History*
Iowa J Hist	*Iowa Journal of History*
Iowa J Hist Pol	*Iowa Journal of History and Politics*
J Am Hist	*Journal of American History*
J Econ Bus Hist	*Journal of Economic and Business History*
J Econ Hist	*Journal of Economic History*
J Hist Ideas	*Journal of the History of Ideas*

J Hist Med	*Journal of the History of Medicine*
J Ill St Hist Soc	*Journal of the Illinois State Historical Society*
J Miss Hist	*Journal of Mississippi History*
J Neg Hist	*Journal of Negro History*
J Pol	*Journal of Politics*
J Pol Econ	*Journal of Political Economy*
J Rel	*Journal of Religion*
J S Hist	*Journal of Southern History*
Kan Hist Q	*Kansas Historical Quarterly*
La Hist	*Louisiana History*
Md Hist Mag	*Maryland Historical Magazine*
Mich Hist	*Michigan History*
Mid-Am	*Mid-America*
Midw J Pol Sci	*Midwest Journal of Political Science*
Midw Q	*Midwest Quarterly*
Mil Aff	*Military Affairs*
Minn Law Rev	*Minnesota Law Review*
Miss Val Hist Rev	*Mississippi Valley Historical Review*
Mo Hist Rev	*Missouri Historical Review*
N C Hist Rev	*North Carolina Historical Review*
N Eng Q	*New England Quarterly*
Neb Hist	*Nebraska History*
N Y Hist	*New York History*
N Y Hist Soc Q	*New York Historical Society Quarterly*
Ohio Arch Hist Pub	*Ohio Archeological and Historical Publications*
Ohio St Arch Hist Q	*Ohio State Archeological and Historical Quarterly*
Ohio Hist	*Ohio History*
Ore Hist Q	*Oregon Historical Quarterly*
Pa Hist	*Pennsylvania History*
Pa Mag	*Pennsylvania Magazine of History and Biography*
Pac Hist Rev	*Pacific Historical Review*
Pac NW Q	*Pacific Northwest Quarterly*
Pap Ill Hist	*Papers in Illinois History*
Partisan Rev	*Partisan Review*
Pitt Law Rev	*University of Pittsburgh Law Review*
Pol Sci Q	*Political Science Quarterly*
Proc Am Ant Soc	*Proceedings, American Antiquarian Society*
Proc Mass Hist Soc	*Proceedings, Massachusetts Historical Society*
Proc N C Hist Assn	*Proceedings, North Carolina Historical Association*
Proc St Hist Soc Wis	*Proceedings, State Historical Society of Wisconsin*
Pub Econ (Berk)	*Publications in Economics*, University of California at Berkeley
Pub Hist (Berk)	*Publications in History*, University of California at Berkeley
Pub Nat Mon Comm	*Publications of the National Monetary Commission*

S Atl Q	*South Atlantic Quarterly*
S Econ J	*Southern Economic Journal*
Soc Sci Q	*Social Science Quarterly*
SW Hist Q	*Southwestern Historical Quarterly*
Stud (Wash)	*Studies,* Washington University
Stud Econ Rel Women	*Studies in Economic Relations of Women*
Stud (Fla)	*Studies,* Florida State University
Stud Hist (Smith)	*Studies in History,* Smith College
Stud Hist Econ Pub Law (Colum)	*Studies in History, Economics, and Public Law,* Columbia University
Stud Hist Pol Sci (Hop)	*Studies in History and Political Science,* Johns Hopkins University
Stud Soc Sci (Ill)	*Studies in the Social Sciences,* University of Illinois
Stud Soc Sci (Minn)	*Studies in the Social Sciences,* University of Minnesota
Tran Ill St Hist Soc	*Transactions, Illinois State Historical Society*
Utah Hist Q	*Utah Historical Quarterly*
Va Mag Hist Biog	*Virginia Magazine of History and Biography*
Wis Mag Hist	*Wisconsin Magazine of History*

Contents

I. General Works

1. Bibliographical Guides and Selected Reference Works

1 ADAMS, James Truslow, and R. V. COLEMAN, eds. *Atlas of American History*. New York, 1943.

2 ADAMS, James Truslow, and R. V. COLEMAN, eds. *Dictionary of American History*. 2nd ed. 5 vols. plus *Index*. New York, 1942.

3 American Historical Association. *Guide to Historical Literature*. New York, 1961.

4 American Historical Association. *Writings on American History*. 46 vols. Washington, 1902–1964.

5 *Biographical Directory of the American Congress, 1774–1961*. Washington, 1961.

6 Bureau of the Census. *Historical Statistics of the United States, Colonial Times to 1957*. Washington, 1960.

7 CARMAN, Harry J., and Arthur W. THOMPSON, eds. *A Guide to the Principal Sources for American Civilization, 1800–1900, in the City of New York: Printed Materials*. New York, 1962.

8 CARRUTH, Gorton, et al. *The Encyclopedia of American Facts and Dates*. 2nd ed. New York, 1959.

9 CLARK, Thomas D., ed. *Travels in the Old South: A Bibliography*. 3 vols. Norman, Okla., 1956–1959. (Volume III covers 1825–1860.)

10 DARGAN, Marion. *Guide to American Biography*. 2 vols. Albuquerque, 1949–1952.

11 DICKINSON, A. T., Jr. *American Historical Fiction*. 2nd ed. New York, 1963.

12 DRIVER, Harold E. *Indians of North America*. Chicago, 1961.†

13 GOHDES, Clarence. *Bibliographical Guide to the Study of the Literature of the U.S.A.* 2nd ed. Durham, N.C., 1963. (Broader than title suggests.)

14 HANDLIN, Oscar, et al. *Harvard Guide to American History*. Cambridge, Mass., 1954.†

15 HART, James D. *The Oxford Companion to American Literature*. 4th ed. New York, 1965.

16 HUBACH, Robert R. *Early Midwestern Travel Narratives: An Annotated Bibliography, 1634–1850*. Detroit, 1961.

17 JOHNSON, Allen, and Dumas MALONE, eds. *Dictionary of American Biography*. 22 vols. New York, 1928–1958.

18 KAPLAN, Louis, et al. *A Bibliography of American Autobiographies*. Madison, Wis., 1961.

19 Library of Congress. *A Guide to the Study of the United States of America*. Washington, 1960.

1 LILLARD, Richard Gordon. *American Life in Autobiography: A Descriptive Guide*. Stanford, 1956.

2 MATTHEWS, William. *American Diaries: An Annotated Bibliography of American Diaries Written Prior to the Year 1861*. Berkeley, 1945.

√3 MORRIS, Richard B., ed. *Encyclopedia of American History*. Rev. ed. New York, 1961.

4 PAULLIN, Charles O. *Atlas of the Historical Geography of the United States*. Washington and New York, 1932.

5 SPILLER, Robert E., et al., eds. *Literary History of the United States: Bibliography*. 3rd ed. New York, 1963. (Covers more than literature.)

6 TAYLOR, Archer, and Bartlett Jere WHITING. *A Dictionary of American Proverbs and Proverbial Phrases, 1820–1880*. Cambridge, Mass., 1958.

2. Collected Works and Other Source Materials

7 ADAMS, John Quincy. *Memoirs of John Quincy Adams*. Ed. by Charles Francis Adams. 12 vols. Philadelphia, 1874–1877.

8 BIRNEY, James Gillespie. *Letters of James Gillespie Birney, 1831–1857*. Ed. by Dwight Lowell Dumond. 2 vols. New York, 1938.

9 BUCHANAN, James. *The Works of James Buchanan*. Ed. by John Bassett Moore. 12 vols. Philadelphia, 1908–1911.

10 CALHOUN, John C. *The Works of John C. Calhoun*. Ed. by Richard K. Crallé. 6 vols. New York, 1854–1857. (1840's not yet reached in publication of *The Papers of John C. Calhoun*, ed. by Robert L. Meriwether and W. Edwin Hemphill, Columbia, S.C., 1959– .)

11 CLAY, Henry. *The Works of Henry Clay*. Ed. by Calvin Colton. 6 vols. New York, 1855. (1840's not yet reached in publication of *The Papers of Henry Clay*, ed. by James F. Hopkins and Mary W. M. Hargreaves, Lexington, Ky., 1959– .)

12 COMMAGER, Henry Steele, ed. *Documents of American History*. 8th ed. New York, 1968.†

13 DANA, Richard Henry, Jr. *The Journal of Richard Henry Dana, Jr*. Ed. by Robert F. Lucid. 3 vols. Cambridge, Mass., 1968.

14 DAVIS, Jefferson. *Jefferson Davis, Constitutionalist: His Letters, Papers, and Speeches*. Ed. by Dunbar Rowland. 10 vols. Jackson, Miss., 1923.

15 DOUGLAS, Stephen A. *The Letters of Stephen A. Douglas*. Ed. by Robert W. Johannsen. Urbana, Ill., 1961.

16 EMERSON, Ralph Waldo. *Journals of Ralph Waldo Emerson, 1820–1876*. Ed. by Edward Waldo Emerson and Waldo Emerson Forbes. 10 vols. Boston, 1909–1914. (Publication under way: *The Journals and Miscellaneous Notebooks of Ralph Waldo Emerson*. Ed. by William H. Gilman, et al. Cambridge, Mass., 1960– .)

1 EMERSON, Ralph Waldo. *The Letters of Ralph Waldo Emerson.* Ed. by Ralph L. Rusk. 6 vols. New York, 1939.

2 HART, Albert Bushnell, ed. *American History Told by Contemporaries.* 5 vols. New York, 1897–1929. (Particularly, Vols. III and IV.)

3 HONE, Philip. *The Diary of Philip Hone, 1828–1851.* Ed. by Allan Nevins. 2nd ed. New York, 1936.

4 HOWE, Samuel Gridley. *Letters and Journals of Samuel Gridley Howe.* Ed. by Laura E. Richards. 2 vols. Boston, 1906–1909.

5 LINCOLN, Abraham. *The Collected Works of Abraham Lincoln.* Ed. by Roy P. Basler, Marion Dolores Pratt, and Lloyd A. Dunlap. 8 vols. plus Index. New Brunswick, N.J., 1953–1955. (There are one-volume paperback selections of Lincoln's works edited by Richard N. Current, Don E. Fehrenbacher, and T. Harry Williams.)

6 MORSE, Samuel F. B. *Samuel F. B. Morse, His Letters and Journals,* Ed. by Edward Lind Morse. 2 vols. Boston, 1914.

7 POTTER, David M., and Thomas G. MANNING, eds. *Nationalism and Sectionalism in America, 1775–1877: Select Problems in Historical Interpretation.* New York, 1949.†

8 RICHARDSON, James D. *A Compilation of the Messages and Papers of the Presidents, 1789–1897.* 10 vols. Washington, 1896–1899. (Particularly, Vols. IV and V.)

9 SEWARD, William H. *The Works of William H. Seward.* Ed. by George E. Baker. 5 vols. Boston, 1853–1884.

10 SIMMS, William Gilmore. *The Letters of William Gilmore Simms.* Ed. by Mary C. Simms Oliphant, Alfred Taylor Odell, and T. C. Duncan Eaves. 5 vols. Columbia, S.C., 1952–1956.

11 STRONG, George Templeton. *The Diary of George Templeton Strong.* Ed. by Allan Nevins and Milton Halsey Thomas. 4 vols. New York, 1952.

12 SUMNER, Charles. *The Works of Charles Sumner.* 15 vols. Boston, 1870–1883.

13 TYLER, Lyon G., ed. *The Letters and Times of the Tylers.* 3 vols. Richmond, 1884–1896.

14 WEBSTER, Daniel. *The Writings and Speeches of Daniel Webster.* National Ed. 18 vols. Boston, 1903.

15 WHITMAN, Walt. *The Collected Writings of Walt Whitman.* Ed. by Gay W. Allen and Sculley Bradley. 8 vols. New York, 1961–1964. (Particularly, Vol. I: *The Correspondence, 1842–1867.* Ed. by Edwin H. Miller.)

16 WHITMAN, Walt. *The Gathering of the Forces.* Ed. by Cleveland Rogers and John Black. 2 vols. New York, 1920. (Editorials, essays, and other material written by Whitman as editor of Brooklyn *Daily Eagle,* 1846–1847.)

3. *Travel Accounts and Other Descriptions*

17 BERGER, Max. *The British Traveller in America, 1836–1860.* New York, 1943. (Scholarly secondary work.)

1 BIRD, Isabella Lucy. *The Englishwoman in America.* London, 1856.

2 BREMER, Fredrika. *The Homes of the New World: Impressions of America.* Trans. by Mary Howitt. 2 vols. New York, 1853. (Prominent Swedish novelist.)

3 BRYANT, William Cullen. *Letters of a Traveller; or, Notes of Things Seen in Europe and America.* New York, 1871.

4 DICKENS, Charles. *American Notes for General Circulation.* 2 vols. London, 1842.

5 GRATTAN, Thomas Colley. *Civilized America.* 2 vols. London, 1859.

6 GREELEY, Horace. *An Overland Journey from New York to San Francisco in the Summer of 1859.* New York, 1860.

7 JOHNSTON, James F. W. *Notes on North America, Agricultural, Economical and Social.* 2 vols. Boston, 1851.

8 LANMAN, Charles. *Adventures in the Wilds of the United States and British American Provinces.* 2 vols. Philadelphia, 1856.

9 LYELL, Sir Charles. *Travels in North America in the Years 1841–1842.* 2 vols. in 1. New York, 1845.

10 LYELL, Sir Charles. *A Second Visit to the United States of North America.* 2 vols. New York, 1849.

11 MACKAY, Alexander. *The Western World; or, Travels in the United States in 1846–47.* 2 vols. Philadelphia, 1849.

12 MACKAY, Charles. *Life and Liberty in America; or, Sketches of a Tour in the United States and Canada, in 1857–8.* 2 vols. New York, 1859.

13 MURRAY, Amelia M. *Letters from the United States, Cuba, and Canada.* New York, 1857.

14 OLMSTED, Frederick Law. *The Cotton Kingdom: A Traveller's Observations on Cotton and Slavery in the American Slave States.* Ed. by Arthur M. Schlesinger. New York, 1953. (First published in 1861, this was Olmsted's own condensation of his three earlier books: *A Journey in the Seaboard Slave States* [1856]; *A Journey through Texas* [1857]; and *A Journey in the Back Country* [1860]. Schlesinger's extensive introduction makes his edition especially valuable.)

15 OLMSTED, Frederick Law. *The Slave States.* Ed. by Harvey Wish. New York, 1959.† (A new and briefer abridgment of the three original books listed above. Good introductory essay.)

16 PULSZKY, Francis and Theresa. *White, Red, Black: Sketches of Society in the United States During the Visit of Their Guest.* 2 vols. New York, 1853. (The "guest" was Louis Kossuth.)

17 RUSSELL, Robert. *North America: Its Agriculture and Climate.* Edinburgh, 1857.

18 STEELE, John. *Across the Plains in 1850.* Ed. by Joseph Schafer. Chicago, 1930. (Not previously published, except serially in a newspaper.)

19 STEEN, Ivan David. "The British Traveler and the American City, 1850–1860." Doctoral dissertation, New York University, 1962.

20 STURGE, Joseph. *A Visit to the United States in 1841.* Boston, 1842. (English Quaker interested especially in the antislavery movement.)

4. *General Studies*

1 AGAR, Herbert. *The Price of Union.* Boston, 1950.†

2 BEARD, Charles A. and Mary R. *The Rise of American Civilization.* 2 vols. New York, 1927.

3 BOORSTIN, Daniel J. *The Americans: The National Experience.* New York, 1965.†

4 BRIGANCE, William N., and Marie Kathryn HOCHMUTH, eds. *A History and Criticism of American Public Address.* 3 vols. New York, 1943–1955.

5 BURGESS, John W. *The Middle Period, 1817–1858.* New York, 1897.

6 CHANNING, Edward. *A History of the United States.* 6 vols. New York, 1905–1925. (Particularly, Vols. V and VI.)

7 CUNLIFFE, Marcus. *Soldiers and Civilians: The Martial Spirit in America, 1775–1865.* Boston, 1968.

8 DEGLER, Carl N. *Out of Our Past: The Forces That Shaped Modern America.* New York, 1959.†

9 DODD, William E. *Expansion and Conflict.* New York, 1915.

10 FEHRENBACHER, Don E. *The Era of Expansion, 1800–1848.* New York, 1969.†

11 MC MASTER, John Bach. *A History of the People of the United States from the Revolution to the Civil War.* 8 vols. New York, 1883–1913. (Particularly, Vols. VII and VIII.)

12 NEVINS, Allan. *Ordeal of the Union.* 4 vols. New York, 1947–1950.† (Preeminent general study of the period 1847–1861. Third and fourth volumes have separate title: *The Emergence of Lincoln.*)

13 NICHOLS, Roy F. *The Stakes of Power, 1845–1877.* New York, 1961.†

14 RHODES, James Ford. *History of the United States from the Compromise of 1850.* 7 vols. New York, 1893–1906. (Particularly, Vols. I–III.)

15 SCHLESINGER, Arthur M., Jr. *The Age of Jackson.* Boston, 1946.† (Later chapters cover period 1840–1860.)

16 SCHOULER, James. *History of the United States of America under the Constitution.* 7 vols. New York, 1880–1913. (Particularly, Vols. IV and V.)

17 SMITH, Elbert B. *The Death of Slavery: The United States, 1837–1865.* Chicago, 1967.†

18 TURNER, Frederick Jackson. *The United States, 1830–1850.* New York, 1935.†

19 VAN DEUSEN, Glyndon G. *The Jacksonian Era, 1828–1848.* New York, 1959.†

20 WILLIAMS, William Appleman. *The Contours of American History.* Cleveland, 1961.†

5. State and Local History
(Listed geographically by states)

1 JORDAN, Holman Drew. "Ten Vermont Towns: Social and Economic Characteristics, 1850–1870." Doctoral dissertation, University of Alabama, 1966.

2 HART, Albert Bushnell, ed. *Commonwealth History of Massachusetts.* 5 vols. New York, 1927–1930. (Particularly, Vol. IV.)

3 GREEN, Constance McLaughlin. *Holyoke, Massachusetts: A Case History of the Industrial Revolution in America.* New Haven, Conn., 1939.

4 COLEMAN, Peter J. *The Transformation of Rhode Island, 1790–1860.* Providence, 1963.

5 MORSE, Jarvis M. *A Neglected Period of Connecticut's History, 1818–1850.* New Haven, Conn., 1933.

6 OSTERWEIS, Rollin G. *Three Centuries of New Haven, 1638–1938.* New Haven, Conn., 1953.

7 FLICK, Alexander C., ed. *History of the State of New York.* 10 vols. New York, 1933–1937. (Particularly, Vols. VI and VII.)

8 STOKES, I. N. Phelps. *The Iconography of Manhattan Island.* 6 vols. New York, 1915–1928. (Unique treasurehouse. Particularly, Vols. III and V.)

9 MC KELVEY, Blake. *Rochester: The Water-Power City, 1812–1854.* Cambridge, Mass., 1945. *Rochester: The Flower City, 1855–1890.* Cambridge, Mass., 1949.

10 BALDWIN, Leland D. *Pittsburgh: The Story of a City.* Pittsburgh, 1937.

11 GREEN, Constance McLaughlin. *Washington, Village and Capital, 1800–1878.* Princeton, 1962.

12 LEFLER, Hugh Talmage, and Albert Ray NEWSOME. *North Carolina: The History of a Southern State.* Rev. ed. Chapel Hill, N.C., 1963.

13 JOHNSON, Guion Griffis. *Ante-Bellum North Carolina: A Social History.* Chapel Hill, N.C., 1937.

14 TAYLOR, Rosser H. *Ante-Bellum South Carolina: A Social and Cultural History.* Chapel Hill, N.C., 1942.

15 BOYD, Minnie Clare. *Alabama in the Fifties: A Social Study.* New York, 1931.

16 JORDAN, Weymouth T. *Ante-Bellum Alabama, Town and Country.* Stud. (Fla), XXVII. Tallahassee, 1957.

17 BOMAN, Martha. "A City of the Old South: Jackson, Mississippi, 1850–1860." *J Miss Hist*, XV(1953):1–32.

18 JAMES, D. Clayton. *Antebellum Natchez.* Baton Rouge, 1968.

19 REINDERS, Robert C. *End of an Era: New Orleans, 1850–1860.* New Orleans, 1964.

20 HAMER, Philip M., ed. *Tennessee: A History, 1673–1932.* 4 vols. New York, 1933.

1 CAPERS, Gerald M. *The Biography of a River Town: Memphis, Its Heroic Age.* Chapel Hill, N.C., 1939.

2 DAVENPORT, F. Garvin. *Ante-Bellum Kentucky: A Social History, 1800–1860.* Oxford, Ohio, 1943.

3 MC REYNOLDS, Edwin C. *Missouri: A History of the Crossroads State.* Norman, Okla., 1962.

4 HUBBART, Henry Clyde. *The Older Middle West, 1840–1880.* New York, 1936. (Ohio, Indiana, and Illinois.)

5 STILL, Bayrd. "Patterns of Mid-Nineteenth Century Urbanization in the Middle West." *Miss Val Hist Rev,* XXVIII(1941):187–206. (On five Great Lakes cities.)

6 WITTKE, Carl F., ed. *The History of the State of Ohio.* 6 vols. Columbus, 1941–1944. (Particularly, Vol. III: Francis P. Weisenburger, *The Passing of the Frontier, 1825–1850* [1941]; and Vol. IV: Eugene H. Roseboom, *The Civil War Era, 1850–1873* [1944].)

7 ESAREY, Logan. *A History of Indiana.* 2 vols. Indianapolis, 1918.

8 THORNBROUGH, Emma Lou. *Indiana in the Civil War Era, 1850–1880.* Indianapolis, 1965. (Vol. III in a projected history of Indiana.)

9 POINSATTE, Charles Robert. "Fort Wayne, Indiana, During the Canal Era, 1828–1855." Doctoral dissertation, University of Notre Dame, 1964.

10 ALVORD, Clarence Walworth, ed. *The Centennial History of Illinois.* 5 vols. Springfield, Ill., 1918–1920. (Particularly, Vol. II: Theodore Calvin Pease, *The Frontier State, 1818–1848* [1918]; and Vol. III: Arthur Charles Cole, *The Era of the Civil War, 1848–1870* [1919].)

11 PIERCE, Bessie Louise. *A History of Chicago.* 3 vols. New York, 1937–1957.

12 CALKINS, Earnest Elmo. *They Broke the Prairie.* New York, 1937. (Early days of Galesburg, Ill., and Knox College.)

13 ANGLE, Paul M. *"Here I Have Lived": A History of Lincoln's Springfield, 1821–1865.* New Brunswick, N.J., 1935.

14 DUNBAR, Willis Frederick. *Michigan: A History of the Wolverine State.* Grand Rapids, Mich., 1965.

15 SCHAFER, Joseph. *Four Wisconsin Counties, Prairie and Forest.* Madison, 1927.

16 CURTI, Merle. *The Making of an American Community: A Case Study of Democracy in a Frontier County.* Stanford, 1959. (Trempealeau County, Wis., 1840–1880.)

17 STILL, Bayrd. *Milwaukee: The History of a City.* Madison, 1948.

18 BLEGEN, Theodore C. *Minnesota: A History of the State.* Minneapolis, 1963.

19 FOLWELL, William W. *A History of Minnesota.* 4 vols. St. Paul, 1921–1930.

20 BROWN, A. Theodore, *Kansas City to 1870.* Columbia, Mo., 1963.

1 RICHARDSON, Rupert Norval. *Texas: The Lone Star State.* 2nd ed. New York, 1958.

2 HOGAN, William Ransom. *The Texas Republic: A Social and Economic History.* Norman, Okla., 1946.

3 SIEGEL, Stanley. *A Political History of the Texas Republic, 1836–1845.* Austin, Texas, 1956.

4 WHEELER, Kenneth William. "Early Urban Development in Texas, 1836–1865." Doctoral dissertation, University of Rochester, 1964.

5 BANCROFT, Hubert Howe. *The Works of Hubert Howe Bancroft.* 39 vols. San Francisco, 1882–1890. (Largely written by uncredited authors in Bancroft's "history factory," this is an enormous storehouse of information, including a 7-volume history of California and a 2-volume history of Oregon.)

6 BEAN, Walton. *California: An Interpretive History.* New York, 1968.

7 CAUGHEY, John Walton. *California.* 2nd ed. New York, 1953.

8 ROLLE, Andrew F. *California: A History.* 2nd ed. New York, 1969.

9 ELLISON, William Henry. *A Self-governing Dominion: California, 1849–1860.* Berkeley, 1950.

10 JOHANSEN, Dorothy O., and Charles M. GATES. *Empire of the Columbia: A History of the Pacific Northwest.* 2nd ed. New York, 1967. (Mainly on Oregon for 1840–1861.)

11 WINTHER, Oscar Osburn. *The Great Northwest: A History.* New York, 1947. (Mainly on Oregon for 1840–1861.)

II. Westward Expansion

1. Bibliography, Historiography, and the Turner Thesis

12 BENSON, Lee. *Turner and Beard: American Historical Writing Reconsidered.* Glencoe, Ill., 1960.†

13 BILLINGTON, Ray Allen. *The American Frontier.* 2nd ed. Washington, 1965. (Service Center for Teachers of History pamphlet.)

14 BILLINGTON, Ray Allen. *Westward Expansion: A History of the American Frontier.* 3rd ed. New York, 1967. (Critical bibliography of 133 pages is the best available.)

15 BILLINGTON, Ray Allen, ed. *The Frontier Thesis: Valid Interpretation of American History?* New York, 1966.† (Anthology of scholarly essays in "American Problem Studies" series.)

16 BURNETTE, O. Lawrence, Jr., ed. *Wisconsin Witness to Frederick Jackson Turner: A Collection of Essays on the Historian and the Thesis.* Madison, Wis., 1961.

17 CHANEY, Homer Campbell, Jr. "The Mexican–United States War, as Seen by Mexican Intellectuals, 1846–1956." Doctoral dissertation, Stanford University, 1959.

18 GRESSLEY, Gene M. "The Turner Thesis—A Problem in Historiography." *Ag Hist,* XXXII(1958):227–249.

1   HAFERKORN, Henry E. *The War with Mexico, 1846–1848: A Select Bibliography on the Causes, Conduct, and Political Aspects of the War.* Washington, 1914.

2   HARSTAD, Peter T., and Richard W. RESH. "The Causes of the Mexican War. A Note on Changing Interpretations." *Ariz W*, VI (1964). 289–302. (Routine summary.)

3   HOFSTADTER, Richard, and Seymour Martin LIPSET, eds. *Turner and the Sociology of the Frontier.* New York, 1968. (Anthology of essays.)

4   NOBLE, David W. *Historians against History: The Frontier Thesis and the National Covenant in American Historical Writing since 1830.* Minneapolis, 1965.†

5   PAUL, Rodman W. "The Mormons as a Theme in Western Historical Writing." *J Am Hist*, LIV(1967):511–523.

6   PIERSON, George W. "The M-Factor in American History." *Am Q*, XIV(1962):275–289. (On mobility.)

7   POMEROY, Earl. "The Changing West." *The Reconstruction of American History.* Ed. by John Higham. New York, 1962.†

8   POTTER, David M. *People of Plenty: Economic Abundance and the American Character.* Chicago, 1954.† (Particularly, Chapter VII: "Abundance and the Frontier Hypothesis.")

9   RUNDELL, Walter, Jr. "Interpretations of the American West, a Descriptive Bibliography." *Ariz W*, III(1961):69–88, 148–168.

10 SMITH, Henry Nash. *Virgin Land: The American West as Symbol and Myth.* Cambridge, Mass., 1950.† (Particularly, the final chapter: "The Myth of the Garden and Turner's Frontier Hypothesis.")

11 TAYLOR, George Rogers, ed. *The Turner Thesis.* Rev. ed. Boston, 1956.† (Anthology of scholarly essays in "Problems in American Civilization" series.)

12 TAYLOR, Philip A. M. "Recent Writing on Utah and the Mormons." *Ariz W*, IV(1962):249–260.

13 TURNER, Frederick Jackson. *The Frontier in American History.* New York, 1920.†

14 WINTHER, Oscar Osburn. *A Classified Bibliography of the Periodical Literature of the Trans-Mississippi West, 1811–1957.* Bloomington, Ind., 1961.

2. *Selected Source Materials*

A. *General*

15 BIEBER, Ralph P., and LeRoy R. HAFEN, eds. *The Southwest Historical Series.* 12 vols. Glendale, Calif., 1931–1943.

16 GRAEBNER, Norman A., ed. *Manifest Destiny.* Indianapolis, 1968.† (Anthology of source materials.)

17 HAFEN, LeRoy R. and Ann W., eds. *The Far West and the Rockies Historical Series, 1820–1875.* 15 vols. Glendale, Calif., 1954–1961.

1   QUAIFE, Milo Milton, ed. *The Diary of James K. Polk During His Presidency, 1845 to 1849.* 4 vols. Chicago, 1910.

B.   Overland Trails and the Early Far West

2   BRYANT, Edwin. *What I Saw in California: Being the Journal of a Tour . . . in the Years 1846, 1847.* New York, 1848.

3   DRUMM, Stella M., ed. *Down the Santa Fe Trail and into New Mexico: The Diary of Susan Shelby Magoffin, 1846–1847.* New Haven, Conn., 1926.†

4   FIELD, Matthew C. *Prairie and Mountain Sketches.* Ed. by Kate L. Gregg and John Francis McDermott. Norman, Okla., 1957.

5   FRÉMONT, John C. *Report of the Exploring Expedition to the Rocky Mountains in the Year 1842, and to Oregon and North California in the Years 1843–44.* Washington, 1845.

6   FULTON, Maurice Garland, ed. *Diary and Letters of Josiah Gregg.* 2 vols. Norman, Okla., 1941–1944. (Santa Fe trader.)

7   GREGG, Josiah. *Commerce of the Prairies.* 2 vols. New York, 1844.†

8   HAMMOND, George P., ed. *The Larkin Papers: Personal, Business, and Official Correspondence of Thomas Oliver Larkin, Merchant and United States Consul in California.* 10 vols. plus Index. Berkeley, 1951–1968.

9   KENDALL, George W. *Narrative of the Texan Santa Fe Expedition.* 2 vols. New York, 1844. (London edition has variant title.)

10   MORGAN, Dale L., ed. *Overland in 1846: Diaries and Letters of the California-Oregon Trail.* 2 vols. Georgetown, Calif., 1963. (Editorial introduction of 104 pages.)

11   NEVINS, Allan, ed. *Narratives of Exploration and Adventure by John Charles Frémont.* New York, 1956. (Selections from Frémont's reports and memoirs.)

12   PALMER, Joel. *Journal of Travels over the Rocky Mountains to the Mouth of the Columbia River Made During the Years 1845 and 1846.* Cincinnati, 1847.

13   RUCKER, Maude A., ed. *The Oregon Trail and Some of Its Blazers.* New York, 1930.

14   SMET, Pierre Jean de. *Oregon Missions and Travels over the Rocky Mountains in 1845–1846.* New York, 1847.

15   SUNDER, John E., ed. *Matt Field on the Santa Fe Trail.* Norman, Okla. 1960. (Journal and newspaper articles, 1839–1841.)

16   THORNTON, J. Q. *Oregon and California in 1848.* 2 vols. New York, 1864.

17   WADE, Mason, ed. *The Journals of Francis Parkman.* 2 vols. New York, 1947. (Vol. II contains Oregon Trail journal.)

C.   Mexican War

18   AMES, George W., Jr., ed. *A Doctor Comes to California: The Diary of John S. Griffin, Assistant Surgeon with Kearny's Dragoons, 1846–1847.* San Francisco, 1943.

1   *An Artillery Officer in the Mexican War, 1846–7: Letters of Robert Anderson.* New York, 1911.

2   CALVIN, Ross, ed. *Lieutenant Emory Reports.* Albuquerque, 1951.

3   COLTON, Walter. *Three Years in California.* New York, 1850.

4   DOUBLEDAY, Rhoda van Bibber Tanner, ed. *Journals of the Late Brevet Major Philip Norbourne Barbour . . . and His Wife, Martha Isabella Hopkins Barbour, Written During the War with Mexico, 1846.* New York, 1936.

5   DOWNEY, Joseph T. *The Cruise of the Portsmouth, 1845–1847: A Sailor's View of the Naval Conquest of California.* Ed. by Howard R. Lamar. New Haven, Conn., 1958.

6   EDWARDS, Frank S. *A Campaign in New Mexico with Colonel Doniphan.* Philadelphia, 1847.

7   GOLDER, Frank Alfred, ed. *The March of the Mormon Battalion from Council Bluffs to California, Taken from the Journal of Henry Standage.* New York, 1928.

8   HUGHES, John T. *Doniphan's Expedition.* Cincinnati, 1848.

9   JAY, William. *A Review of the Causes and Consequences of the Mexican War.* Boston, 1849. (Abolitionist, son of John Jay.)

10 MYERS, William Starr, ed. *The Mexican War Diary of George B. McClellan.* Princeton, 1917.

11 SMITH, George Winston, and Charles JUDAH, eds. *Chronicle of the Gringos: The U.S. Army in the Mexican War, 1846–1848, Accounts of Eye-witnesses and Combatants.* Albuquerque, 1968.

D.   The Gold Rush

12 AUDUBON, John J. *Audubon's Western Journal, 1849–1850.* Ed. by Frank Heywood Hodder. Cleveland, 1906.

13 BUFFUM, E. Gould. *Six Months in the Gold Mines.* Philadelphia, 1850. (On the 1848 rush.)

14 DELANO, Alonzo. *Life on the Plains and among the Diggings.* Auburn, N.Y., 1854.

15 HELPER, Hinton Rowan. *The Land of Gold: Reality versus Fiction.* Baltimore, 1855. (A sour view.)

16 MARRYAT, Frank. *Mountains and Molehills.* New York, 1855.†

17 MORGAN, Dale L., ed. *Overland Diary of James A. Pritchard, from Kentucky to California in 1849.* Denver, 1959. (Extensive editorial material.)

18 POTTER, David M., ed. *Trail to California: The Overland Journal of Vincent Geiger and Wakeman Bryarly.* New Haven, Conn., 1945.† (Long and informative introduction.)

19 READ, Georgia Willis, and Ruth GAINES, eds. *Gold Rush: The Journals, Drawings, and Other Papers of J. Goldsborough Bruff . . . April 2, 1849–July 20, 1851.* 2 vols. New York, 1944.

20 ROYCE, Sara. *A Frontier Lady: Recollections of the Gold Rush and Early California.* Ed. by Ralph Henry Gabriel. New Haven, Conn., 1932.

1   SCAMEHORN, Howard L., ed. *The Buckeye Rovers in the Gold Rush.* Athens, Ohio, 1965. (Two diaries.)

2   TAYLOR, Bayard. *Eldorado; or, Adventures in the Path of Empire.* 2 vols. London, 1850.

3   WHEAT, Carl I., ed. *The Shirley Letters from the California Mines, 1851–1852.* New York, 1949. (First published, serially, in 1854–1855. "Dame Shirley" was the pseudonym of Louise Amelia Knapp Smith Clappe.)

4   WYMAN, Walker D., ed. *California Emigrant Letters.* New York, 1952.

E.   Other Special Topics

5   BROOKS, Juanita, ed. *On the Mormon Frontier: The Diary of Hosea Stout, 1844–1861.* 2 vols. Salt Lake City, 1964.

6   BURTON, Richard F. *The City of Saints and Across the Rocky Mountains to California.* London, 1861.

7   DONALDSON, Thomas. *The Public Domain: Its History with Statistics.* Washington, 1884.

8   EASTMAN, Mary. *Dahcotah; or, Life and Legends of the Sioux around Fort Snelling.* Minneapolis, 1962. (Originally published in 1849.)

9   EATON, Clement, ed. "Frontier Life in Southern Arizona, 1858–1861." *SW Hist Q,* XXXVI(1933):173–192.

10 FOREMAN, Grant, ed. *A Pathfinder in the Southwest: The Itinerary of Lieutenant A. W. Whipple During His Explorations for a Railway Route from Fort Smith to Los Angeles in the Years 1853 & 1854.* Norman, Okla., 1941.

11 LOWE, Percival G. *Five Years a Dragoon.* Ed. by Don Russell. Norman, Okla., 1965. (On the 1850's; first published in 1906.)

12 MORGAN, Lewis Henry. *The Indian Journals, 1859–62.* Ed. by Leslie A. White. Ann Arbor, Mich., 1959. (Kansas-Nebraska region.)

13 MULDER, William, and A. Russell MORTENSEN, eds. *Among the Mormons: Historic Accounts by Contemporary Observers.* New York, 1958.

14 QUAIFE, Milo Milton. *The Movement for Statehood, 1845–1846; The Convention of 1846; The Struggle over Ratification, 1846–1847; The Attainment of Statehood.* Madison, Wis., 1918–1928. (4-volume series of documents.)

15 WALKER, William. *The War in Nicaragua.* New York, 1860.

16 *William Clayton's Journal.* Salt Lake City, 1921. (Mormon migration of 1847.)

3. General Studies

17 BENDER, Averam B. *The March of Empire: Frontier Defense in the Southwest, 1848–1860.* Lawrence, Kan., 1952.

1 BILLINGTON, Ray Allen. *America's Frontier Heritage*. New York, 1966.†

2 BILLINGTON, Ray Allen. *The Far Western Frontier, 1830–1860*. New York, 1956.†

3 BILLINGTON, Ray Allen. *Westward Expansion*. See 8.14.

4 DE VOTO, Bernard. *The Year of Decision*. Boston, 1943.†

5 GARRISON, George Pierce. *Westward Extension, 1841–1850*. New York, 1906.

6 GOETZMANN, William H. *When the Eagle Screamed: The Romantic Horizon in American Diplomacy, 1800–1860*. New York, 1966.†

7 GOODWIN, Cardinal. *The Trans-Mississippi West (1803–1853)*. New York. 1922.

8 GREEVER, William S. *The Bonanza West: The Story of the Western Mining Rushes, 1848–1900*. Norman, Okla., 1963.

9 HAWGOOD, John A. *America's Western Frontiers: The Exploration and Settlement of the Trans-Mississippi West*. New York, 1967.

10 LAVENDER, David. *Land of Giants: The Drive to the Pacific Northwest, 1750–1950*. Garden City, N.Y., 1958.

11 MC CALEB, Walter F. *The Conquest of the West*. New York, 1947.

12 MC ELROY, Robert McNutt. *The Winning of the Far West*. New York, 1914.

13 PAUL, Rodman W. *Mining Frontiers of the Far West, 1848–1880*. New York, 1963.†

4. Exploration and Settlement

14 CHITTENDEN, Hiram Martin. *The American Fur Trade of the Far West*. 3 vols. New York, 1902. (Final chapters of this standard work extend into 1840's.)

15 CLELAND, Robert Glass. *This Reckless Breed of Men: The Trappers and Fur Traders of the Southwest*. New York, 1950.

16 DICK, Everett. *The Sod-House Frontier, 1854–1890*. New York, 1937.

17 GAMBLE, Richard Dalzell. "Garrison Life at Frontier Military Posts, 1830–1860." Doctoral dissertation, University of Oklahoma, 1956.

18 GHENT, W. J. *The Road to Oregon: A Chronicle of the Great Emigrant Trail*. New York, 1929.

19 GOETZMANN, William H. *Army Exploration in the American West, 1803–1863*. New Haven, Conn., 1959.†

20 GOETZMANN, William H. *Exploration and Empire: The Explorer and the Scientist in the Winning of the American West*. New York, 1966.

21 GOETZMANN, William H. "The Mountain Man as Jacksonian Man." *Am Q*, XV(1963):402–415.

1 HOLLON, W. Eugene. *Beyond the Cross Timbers: The Travels of Randolph B. Marcy, 1812–1887.* Norman, Okla., 1955.

2 LARPENTEUR, Charles. *Forty Years a Fur Trader on the Upper Missouri . . . 1833–1872.* Ed. by Elliot Coues, 2 vols. New York, 1898.

3 LAVENDER, David. *Westward Vision: The Story of the Oregon Trail.* New York, 1963. (Largely pre-1840.)

4 MONAGHAN, Jay. *The Overland Trail.* Indianapolis, 1947.

5 PADEN, Irene D. *The Wake of the Prairie Schooner.* New York, 1943.

6 PARKMAN, Francis. *The Oregon Trail,* New York, 1849.† (Original title was *The California and Oregon Trail.* Adventurous journey in 1846, mostly on the Great Plains.)

7 STEGNER, Wallace. *The Gathering of Zion: The Story of the Mormon Trail.* New York, 1964.

8 STEWART, George R. *The California Trail: An Epic with Many Heroes.* New York, 1962.

9 STEWART, George R. *Ordeal by Hunger: The Story of the Donner Party.* Boston, 1960.

10 SUNDER, John E. *The Fur Trade on the Upper Missouri, 1840–1865.* Norman, Okla., 1965.

11 THROCKMORTON, Arthur L. *Oregon Argonauts: Merchant Adventurers on the Western Frontier.* Portland, Ore., 1961.

12 WALLACE, Edward S. *The Great Reconnaissance: Soldiers, Artists, and Scientists on the Frontier, 1848–1861.* Boston, 1955.

5. The Western Indians

13 ANSON, Bert. "Variations of the Indian Conflict: The Effects of the Emigrant Indian Removal Policy, 1830–1854." *Mo Hist Rev,* LIX(1964): 64–89.

14 BAILEY, Lynn R. *The Long Walk: A History of the Navajo Wars, 1848–68.* Los Angeles, 1964.

15 BERKHOFER, Robert F., Jr. *Salvation and the Savage: An Analysis of Protestant Missions and American Indian Response, 1787–1862.* Lexington, Ky., 1965.

16 BERTHRONG, Donald J. *The Southern Cheyennes.* Norman, Okla., 1963.

17 BRANDON, William. *The American Heritage Book of Indians,* New York, 1961.

18 BURNS, Robert I. *The Jesuits and the Indian Wars of the Northwest.* New Haven, Conn., 1966.

19 DALE, Edward Everett. *The Indians of the Southwest: A Century of Development under the United States.* Norman, Okla., 1949.

20 FOREMAN, Grant. *The Five Civilized Tribes.* Norman, Okla., 1934.

1 HOOPES, Alban W. *Indian Affairs and Their Administration, with Special Reference to the Far West, 1849–1860.* Philadelphia, 1932.

2 HYDE, George E. *Pawnee Indians.* Denver, 1951.

3 LEWIT, Robert T. "Indian Missions and Antislavery Sentiment: A Conflict of Evangelical and Humanitarian Ideals." *Miss Val Hist Rev,* L(1963):39–55.

4 PARKMAN, Francis. *The Oregon Trail.* See 14:6.

5 PRUCHA, Francis P. "Indian Removal and the Great American Desert." *Ind Mag Hist,* LIX(1963):299–322.

6 RICHARDSON, Rupert Norval. *The Comanche Barrier to South Plains Settlement.* Glendale, Calif., 1933.

7 TRENHOLM, Virginia Cole, and Maurine CARLEY. *The Shoshonis, Sentinels of the Rockies.* Norman, Okla., 1964.

8 UTLEY, Robert M. *Frontiersmen in Blue: The United States Army and the Indian, 1848–1865.* New York, 1967.

9 WALLACE, Ernest, and Edward Adamson HOEBEL. *The Comanches, Lords of the South Plains.* Norman, Okla., 1952.

10 WARDELL, Morris L. *A Political History of the Cherokee Nation, 1838–1907.* Norman, Okla., 1938.

6. *Territorial Government and State-Making*
(For Kansas, see 90.18–91.18.)

11 ANDERSON, William. *A History of the Constitution of Minnesota. Stud Soc Sci* (Minn). Minneapolis, 1921.

12 CASH, W. T., and Dorothy DODD. *Florida Becomes a State.* Tallahassee, 1945. (Partly documents.)

13 CREER, Leland H. *Utah and the Nation.* Seattle, 1929.

14 EBLEN, Jack Ericson. *The First and Second United States Empires: Governors and Territorial Government, 1784–1912.* Pittsburgh, 1968.

15 FURNISS, Norman F. *The Mormon Conflict, 1850–1859.* New Haven, Conn., 1960.†

16 GOODWIN, Cardinal. *The Establishment of State Government in California, 1846–1850.* New York, 1914.

17 GOWER, Calvin W. "Kansas Territory and the Pike's Peak Gold Rush: Governing the Gold Region." *Kan Hist Q,* XXXII(1966):289–313.

18 GRIVAS, Theodore. *Military Governments in California, 1846–1850.* Glendale, Calif., 1963.

19 LAMAR, Howard R. *Dakota Territory, 1861–1889: A Study of Frontier Politics.* New Haven, Conn., 1956.† (Introduction surveys earlier territorial policies.)

20 LAMAR, Howard R. *The Far Southwest, 1846–1912: A Territorial History.* New Haven, Conn., 1966.†

1 SIMMS, Henry H. "The Controversy over the Admission of the State of Oregon." *Miss Val Hist Rev*, XXXII(1945):355–374.

2 STILL, Bayrd. "State-Making in Wisconsin, 1846–48." *Wis Mag Hist*, XX(1936):34–59.

7. Western Land

3 BOGUE, Allan G. "The Iowa Claim Clubs: Symbol and Substance." *Miss Val Hist Rev*, XLV(1958):231–253. (New light on squatters. Reprinted in Carstensen book below.)

4 CARSTENSEN, Vernon, ed. *The Public Lands: Studies in the History of the Public Domain*. Madison, Wis., 1963.

5 GATES, Paul Wallace. "The Adjudication of Spanish-Mexican Land Claims in California." *Hunt Lib Q*, XXI(1958):213–236.

6 GATES, Paul Wallace. "California's Embattled Settlers." *Calif Hist Soc Q*, XLI(1962):99–130.

7 GATES, Paul Wallace. *Fifty Million Acres: Conflicts over Kansas Land Policy, 1854–1890*. Ithaca, N.Y., 1954.†

8 GATES, Paul Wallace. *The Illinois Central Railroad and Its Colonization Work*. Cambridge, Mass., 1934.

9 GATES, Paul Wallace. "The Struggle for Land and the 'Irrepressible Conflict.'" *Pol Sci Q*, LXVI(1951):248–271.

10 HIBBARD, Benjamin H. *A History of Public Land Policies*. New York, 1924.†

11 MALIN, James C. *The Nebraska Question, 1852–1854*. Lawrence, Kan., 1953.

12 ROBBINS, Roy M. *Our Landed Heritage: The Public Domain, 1776–1936*. Princeton, 1942.†

13 STEPHENSON, George M. *The Political History of the Public Lands from 1840 to 1862*. Boston, 1917.

14 SWIERENGA, Robert P. *Pioneers and Profits: Land Speculation on the Iowa Frontier*. Ames, Iowa, 1968. (Heavily statistical. Speculation proved both profitable and socially useful.)

15 WILLIAMS, Elgin. *The Animating Pursuits of Speculation: Land Traffic in the Annexation of Texas*. New York, 1949.

16 WOLFF, Gerald. "The Slavocracy and the Homestead Problem of 1854." *Ag Hist*, XL(1966):101–111.

17 YOUNG, Mary Elizabeth. *Redskins, Ruffleshirts, and Rednecks: Indian Allotments in Alabama and Mississippi, 1830–1860*. Norman, Okla., 1961.

18 ZAHLER, Helene Sara. *Eastern Workingmen and National Land Policy 1829–1862*. New York, 1941.

8. Western Transportation and Communication
(See also 45.15–48.20.)

19 BANNING, William and George Hugh. *Six Horses*. New York, 1930. (California staging.)

1 CHAPMAN, Arthur. *The Pony Express: The Record of a Romantic Adventure in Business*. New York, 1932.

2 CLARK, Arthur H. *The Clipper Ship Era . . . 1843–1869*. New York, 1911.

3 CONKLING, Roscoe P. and Margaret B. *The Butterfield Overland Mail, 1857–1869*. 3 vols. Glendale, Calif., 1947.

4 DUFFUS, R. L. *The Santa Fe Trail*. New York, 1930.

5 FOWLER, Harlan D. *Camels to California*. Stanford, 1950.

6 HAFEN, LeRoy R. *The Overland Mail, 1849–1869*. Cleveland, 1926.

7 HUNGERFORD, Edward. *Wells Fargo: Advancing the American Frontier*. New York, 1949.

8 JACKSON, W. Turrentine. *Wagon Roads West: A Study of Federal Road Surveys and Construction in the Trans-Mississippi West, 1846–1869*. Berkeley, 1952.†

9 KEMBLE, John H. *The Panama Route, 1848–1869*. Berkeley, 1943.

10 LEWIS, Oscar. *Sea Routes to the Gold Fields: The Migration by Water to California in 1849–1852*. New York, 1949.

11 MAC MULLEN, Jerry. *Paddlewheel Days in California*. Stanford, 1944.

12 MOODY, Ralph. *Stagecoach West*. New York, 1967.

13 RIESENBERG, Felix, Jr. *Golden Gate: The Story of San Francisco Harbor*. New York, 1940.

14 RUSSEL, Robert R. *Improvement of Communication with the Pacific Coast as an Issue in American Policies, 1783–1864*. Cedar Rapids, Iowa, 1948.

15 SETTLE, Raymond W. and Mary Lund. *Saddles and Spurs: The Pony Express Saga*. Harrisburg, Pa., 1955.

16 SETTLE, Raymond W. and Mary Lund. *War Drums and Wagon Wheels: The Story of Russell, Majors and Waddell*. Lincoln, Neb., 1966.

17 WALKER, Henry Pickering. *The Wagonmasters: High Plains Freighting from the Earliest Days of the Santa Fe Trail to 1880*. Norman, Okla., 1966.

18 WINTHER, Oscar Osburn. *Express and Stagecoach Days in California*. Stanford, 1936.

19 WINTHER, Oscar Osburn. *The Old Oregon Country: A History of Frontier Trade, Transportation, and Travel*. Stanford, 1950.

20 WYMAN, Walker D. "Freighting: A Big Business on the Santa Fe Trail" and "The Military Phase of Santa Fe Freighting, 1846–1865." *Kan Hist Q*, I(1931–1932):17–27, 415–428.

9. Manifest Destiny

21 ADAMS, Ephraim Douglass. *The Power of Ideals in American History*. New Haven, Conn., 1913.

22 CURTI, Merle. "Young America." *Am Hist Rev*, XXXII(1926):34–55.

23 FOWLER, Nolan. "Territorial Expansion—A Threat to the Republic?" *Pac NW Q*, LIII(1962):34–42.

1   FRANKLIN, John Hope. "The Southern Expansionists of 1846." *J S Hist*, XXV(1959):323–338.

2   FRITZ, Henry E. "Nationalistic Response to Frontier Expansion." *Mid-Am*, LI(1969):227–243.

3   GAWRONSKI, Donald Vincent. "Transcendentalism: An Ideological Basis for Manifest Destiny." Doctoral dissertation, St. Louis University, 1964.

4   GIBSON, George H. "Opinion in North Carolina Regarding the Acquisition of Texas and Cuba, 1835–1855." *N C Hist Rev*, XXXVII(1960):1–21, 185–201.

5   HAWGOOD, John A. "Manifest Destiny." *British Essays in American History*. Ed. by H. C. Allen and C. P. Hill. New York, 1957.

6   MERK, Frederick. *Manifest Destiny and Mission in American History: A Reinterpretation*. New York, 1963.†

7   MERK, Frederick. *The Monroe Doctrine and American Expansionism, 1843–1849*. New York, 1966.

8   MILES, Edwin A. "Fifty-Four Forty or Fight—An American Political Legend." *Miss Val Hist Rev*, XLIV(1957):291–309.

9   PRATT, Julius W. "The Ideology of American Expansionism." *Essays in Honor of William E. Dodd*. Ed. by Avery Craven. Chicago, 1935.

10 VEVIER, Charles. "American Continentalism: An Idea of Expansion, 1845–1910." *Am Hist Rev*, LXV(1960):323–335.

11 WEINBERG, Albert K. *Manifest Destiny*. Baltimore, 1935.†

10. Texas and the Mexican War

12 ADAMS, Ephraim Douglass. *British Interests and Activities in Texas, 1838–1846*. Baltimore, 1910.

13 BILL, Alfred Hoyt. *Rehearsal for Conflict: The War with Mexico, 1846–1848*. New York, 1947.

14 BINKLEY, William C. *The Expansionist Movement in Texas, 1836–1850. Pub Hist* (Berk), XIII. Berkeley, 1925.

15 BOURNE, Edward Gaylord. "The Proposed Absorption of Mexico in 1847–48." In his *Essays in Historical Criticism*. New York, 1901.

16 BRAUER, Kinley J. *Cotton versus Conscience: Massachusetts Whig Politics and Southwestern Expansion, 1843–1848*. Lexington, Ky., 1967.

17 ELLSWORTH, Clayton Sumner. "The American Churches and the Mexican War." *Am Hist Rev*, XLV(1940):301–326.

18 FULLER, John D. P. *The Movement for the Acquisition of All Mexico, 1846–1848. Stud Hist Pol Sci* (Hop), LIV. Baltimore, 1936.

19 HENRY, Robert Selph. *The Story of the Mexican War*. Indianapolis, 1950.

20 HINE, Robert V. *Bartlett's West: Drawing the Mexican Boundary*. New Haven, Conn., 1968.

21 HORGAN, Paul. *Great River: The Rio Grande*. 2 vols. New York, 1954.†

1 LAVENDER, David. *Climax at Buena Vista: The American Campaigns in Northeastern Mexico, 1846–47.* Philadelphia, 1966.

2 LOFGREN, Charles A. "Force and Diplomacy, 1846–1848: The View from Washington." *Mil Aff*, XXXI(1967):57–64.

3 LOOMIS, Noel M. *The Texan–Santa Fe Pioneers.* Norman, Okla., 1958. (The ill-fated Santa Fe expedition of 1841.)

4 MERK, Frederick. "A Safety Valve Thesis and Texan Annexation." *Miss Val Hist Rev*, XLIX(1962):413–436.

5 NANCE, Joseph Milton. *After San Jacinto: The Texas-Mexican Frontier, 1836–1841,* and *Attack and Counterattack: The Texas-Mexican Frontier, 1842.* Austin, 1963–1964.

6 PITCHFORD, Louis Cleveland, Jr. "The Diplomatic Representatives from the United States to Mexico from 1836 to 1848." Doctoral dissertation, University of Colorado, 1965.

7 PRICE, Glenn W. *Origins of the War with Mexico: The Polk-Stockton Intrigue.* Austin, 1967. (Extremely critical of Polk, the United States, and American historians.)

8 REEVES, Jesse S. *American Diplomacy under Tyler and Polk.* Baltimore, 1907.

9 RIVES, George L. *The United States and Mexico, 1821–1848.* 2 vols. New York, 1913.

10 RUIZ, Ramón Eduardo, ed. *The Mexican War—Was It Manifest Destiny?* New York, 1963.† (Anthology of essays and passages from books in "American Problem Studies" series.)

11 SCHMITZ, Joseph William. *Texan Statecraft, 1836–1845.* San Antonio, 1941.

12 SEARS, Louis M. "Nicholas P. Trist, a Diplomat with Ideals." *Miss Val Hist Rev*, XI(1924):85–98.

13 SINGLETARY, Otis A. *The Mexican War.* New York, 1960.†

14 SMITH, Justin H. *The Annexation of Texas.* New York, 1911.

15 SMITH, Justin H. *The War with Mexico.* 2 vols. New York, 1919. (The most exhaustive study.)

16 STENBERG, Richard R. "Failure of Polk's Mexican War Intrigue of 1845." *Pac Hist Rev*, IV(1935):39–68.

17 STEPHENSON, Nathaniel W. *Texas and the Mexican War: A Chronicle of the Winning of the Southwest.* New Haven, Conn., 1921.

18 TUTOROW, Norman E. "Whigs of the Old Northwest and the Mexican War." Doctoral dissertation, Stanford University, 1967.

19 WILLIAMS, Elgin. *The Animating Pursuits of Speculation.* See 16.15.

11. Acquisition of Oregon and California

20 BROOKE, George M., Jr. "The Vest Pocket War of Commodore Jones." *Pac Hist Rev*, XXXI(1962):217–233.

21 CLELAND, Robert Glass. *Early Sentiment for the Annexation of California . . . 1835 to 1846.* Austin, 1915.

1 COOKE, Philip St. George. *The Conquest of New Mexico and California.* New York, 1878. (Commander of the Mormon Battalion.)

2 CRAMER, Richard S. "British Magazines and the Oregon Question." *Pac Hist Rev*, XXXII(1963):369–382.

3 GALBRAITH, John S. *The Hudson's Bay Company as an Imperial Factor, 1821–1869.* Berkeley, 1957.

4 GRAEBNER, Norman A. *Empire on the Pacific: A Study in American Continental Expansion.* New York, 1955.†

5 GRAEBNER, Norman A. "Politics and the Oregon Compromise." *Pac NW Q*, LII(1961):7–14.

6 HAWGOOD, John A. "John C. Frémont and the Bear Flag Revolution: A Reappraisal." *Hist Soc S Calif Q*, XLIV(1962):67–96. (Includes a useful bibliography.)

7 HAWGOOD, John A. "The Pattern of Yankee Infiltration in Mexican Alta California, 1821–1846." *Pac Hist Rev*, XXVII(1958):27–37.

8 HUSSEY, John A. "The Origin of the Gillespie Mission." *Calif Hist Soc Q*, XIX(1940):43–58.

9 JACOBS, Melvin C. *Winning Oregon.* Caldwell, Idaho, 1938.

10 JONES, Wilbur D. *Lord Aberdeen and the Americas.* Athens, Ga., 1958. (British Foreign Secretary, 1841–1848.)

11 JONES, Wilbur D., and J. Chal VINSON. "British Preparedness and the Oregon Settlement." *Pac Hist Rev*, XXII(1953):353–364.

12 KNAPP, Frank A., Jr. "The Mexican Fear of Manifest Destiny in California." *Essays in Mexican History.* Ed. by Thomas E. Cotner and Carlos E. Castañeda. Austin, 1958.

13 MC CABE, James O. "Arbitration and the Oregon Question." *Can Hist Rev*, XLI(1960):308–327.

14 MARTIN, Thomas P. "Free Trade and the Oregon Question, 1842–1846." *Facts and Factors in Economic History: Articles by Former Students of Edwin Francis Gay.* Cambridge, Mass., 1932.

15 MERK, Frederick. *The Oregon Question: Essays in Anglo-American Diplomacy and Politics.* Cambridge, Mass., 1967. (The leading authority.)

16 PRATT, Julius W. "James K. Polk and John Bull." *Can Hist Rev*, XXIV (1943):341–349.

17 ROYCE, Josiah. *California, from the Conquest in 1846 to the Second Vigilance Committee in San Francisco: A Study of American Character.* Boston, 1886. (Durable classic.)

18 SCHERER, James A. B. *Thirty-First Star.* New York, 1942.

19 STENBERG, Richard R. "Polk and Frémont, 1845–1846." *Pac Hist Rev*, VII(1938):211–227.

20 TAYS, George. "Frémont Had No Secret Instructions." *Pac Hist Rev*, IX(1940):157–171.

21 VAN ALSTYNE, Richard W. "International Rivalries in the Pacific Northwest." *Ore Hist Q*, XLVI(1945):185–218.

22 WOODWARD, Arthur. *Lances at San Pascual.* San Francisco, 1948.

12. Gold Rush

1 BIEBER, Ralph P. "California Gold Mania." *Miss Val Hist Rev,* XXXV(1948):3–28.

2 CAUGHEY, John Walton. *Gold Is the Cornerstone.* Berkeley, 1948.

3 CAUGHEY, John Walton, ed. *Rushing for Gold.* Berkeley, 1949. (Anthology of essays.)

4 CLELAND, Robert Glass. *The Cattle on a Thousand Hills: Southern California, 1850–1880.* San Marino, Calif., 1941.

5 COY, Owen C. *The Great Trek.* Los Angeles, 1931.

6 HOWE, Octavius Thorndike. *Argonauts of '49: History and Adventures of the Emigrant Companies from Massachusetts, 1849–1850.* Cambridge, Mass., 1923. (Emphasizes Cape Horn route.)

7 JACKSON, Joseph H. *Anybody's Gold: The Story of California's Mining Towns.* New York, 1941.

8 KEMBLE, John H. *The Panama Route.* See 17.9.

9 LEWIS, Oscar. *Sea Routes to the Gold Fields.* See 17.10.

10 LEWIS, Oscar. *Sutter's Fort: Gateway to the Gold Fields.* Englewood Cliffs, N. J., 1966.

11 PAUL, Rodman W. *California Gold.* Cambridge, Mass., 1947.† (The most scholarly general study.)

12 RIESENBERG, Felix, Jr. *Golden Gate.* See 17.13.

13 ROSKE, Ralph J. "The World Impact of the California Gold Rush, 1849–1857." *Ariz W,* V(1963):187–232.

14 ROYCE, Josiah. *California.* See 20.17.

15 SHINN, Charles Howard. *Mining Camps: A Study in American Frontier Government.* New York, 1885.

16 STEWART, George R. *Committee of Vigilance: Revolution in San Francisco, 1851.* Boston, 1964.

13. The Mormons

17 ANDERSON, Nels. *Desert Saints: The Mormon Frontier in Utah.* Chicago, 1942.†

18 ARRINGTON, Leonard J. *Great Basin Kingdom: An Economic History of the Latter-Day Saints, 1830–1900.* Cambridge, Mass., 1958.†

19 BROOKS, Juanita. *The Mountain Meadows Massacre.* Rev. ed. Norman, Okla., 1962.

20 CREER, Leland H. *The Founding of an Empire: The Exploration and Colonization of Utah, 1776–1856.* Salt Lake City, 1947.

21 CREER, Leland H. *Utah and the Nation.* See 15.13.

22 FIFE, Austin and Alta. *Saints of Sage and Saddle: Folklore among the Mormons.* Bloomington, Ind., 1956.

1 FLANDERS, Robert Bruce. *Nauvoo: Kingdom on the Mississippi.* Urbana, Ill., 1965.

2 FURNISS, Norman F. *The Mormon Conflict.* See 15.15.

3 HANSEN, Klaus J. *Quest for Empire: The Political Kingdom of God and the Council of Fifty in Mormon History.* East Lansing, 1967.

4 LARSON, Gustive O. "The Mormon Reformation." *Utah Hist Q,* XXVI(1958):45–63.

5 LARSON, Gustive O. *Prelude to the Kingdom: Mormon Desert Conquest.* Francestown, N.H., 1947.

6 LINN, William Alexander. *The Story of the Mormons.* New York, 1902.

7 MAC KINNON, William P. "The Buchanan Spoils System and the Utah Expedition." *Utah Hist Q,* XXXI(1963):127–150.

8 MORGAN, Dale L. "The State of Deseret." *Utah Hist Q,* VIII(1940):65–251. (Virtually a book, half documentary.)

9 MULDER, William. *Homeward to Zion: The Mormon Migration from Scandinavia.* Minneapolis, 1957.

10 NEFF, Andrew Love. *History of Utah, 1847 to 1869.* Ed. by Leland H. Creer. Salt Lake City, 1940.

11 O'DEA, Thomas F. *The Mormons.* Chicago, 1957.†

12 POLL, Richard D. "The Mormon Question Enters National Politics, 1850–1856." *Utah Hist Q,* XXV(1957):117–131.

13 QUAIFE, Milo Milton. *The Kingdom of Saint James: A Narrative of the Mormons.* New Haven, Conn., 1930. (A schismatic Mormon community.)

14 ROBERTS, B. H. *A Comprehensive History of the Church of Jesus Christ of Latter-Day Saints.* 6 vols. Salt Lake City, 1930.

15 STENHOUSE, T. B. H. *The Rocky Mountain Saints.* New York, 1873.

16 TAYLOR, Philip A. M. *Expectations Westward: The Mormons and the Emigration of Their British Converts in the Nineteenth Century.* Edinburgh, 1965.

17 WEST, Ray B., Jr. *Kingdom of the Saints: The Story of Brigham Young and the Mormons.* New York, 1957.

14. Other Frontiers

18 EMMET, Chris. *Fort Union and the Winning of the Southwest.* Norman, Okla., 1965.

19 GLUEK, Alvin C., Jr. *Minnesota and the Manifest Destiny of the Canadian Northwest.* Toronto, 1965.

20 GRAEBNER, Norman A. "Nebraska's Missouri River Frontier, 1854–1860." *Neb Hist,* XLII(1961):213–235.

21 HAFEN, LeRoy R., and Francis Marion YOUNG. *Fort Laramie and the Pageant of the West, 1834–1890.* Glendale, Calif., 1938.

22 KANE, Lucile M. *The Waterfall That Built a City: The Falls of St. Anthony in Minneapolis.* St. Paul, 1966.

1 LAVENDER, David. *Bent's Fort*. New York, 1954.

2 LOCKWOOD, Frank C. *Pioneer Days in Arizona*. New York, 1932.

3 LYMAN, George D. *The Saga of the Comstock Lode*. New York, 1934.

4 MIRSKY, Jeannette. *Elisha Kent Kane and the Seafaring Frontier*. Boston, 1954. (Arctic exploration.)

5 RICHARDSON, Rupert Norval. *The Frontier of Northwest Texas, 1846 to 1876*. Glendale, Calif., 1963.

6 ROBERTSON, Frank C. *Fort Hall: Gateway to the Oregon Country*. New York, 1963.

7 SMITH, Grant H. *The History of the Comstock Lode, 1850–1920*. Reno, Nev., 1943.

8 TYLER, David B. *The Wilkes Expedition: The First United States Exploration Expedition (1838–1842)*. Philadelphia, 1968.

9 WEBB, Walter Prescott. *The Great Plains*. Boston, 1931.†

15. *Expansionism in the 1850's*

10 CALDWELL, Robert Granville. *The López Expeditions to Cuba, 1848–1851*. Princeton, 1915.

11 CARR, Albert Z. *The World and William Walker*. New York, 1963.

12 CRENSHAW, Ollinger. "The Knights of the Golden Circle: The Career of George Bickley." *Am Hist Rev*, XLVII(1941):23–50.

13 FAULK, Odie B. *Too Far North, Too Far South*. Los Angeles, 1967. (Survey of United States–Mexican boundary, 1848–1853.)

14 FONER, Philip S. *A History of Cuba and Its Relations with the United States*. 2 vols. New York, 1962–1963. (Particularly, Vol. II.)

15 FORNELL, Earl W. "Texans and Filibusters in the 1850's." *SW Hist Q*, LIX(1956):411–428.

16 GARBER, Paul Neff. *The Gadsden Treaty*. Philadelphia, 1923.

17 RAUCH, Basil. *American Interest in Cuba, 1848–1855*. New York, 1948.

18 SCHMIDT, Louis Bernard. "Manifest Opportunity and the Gadsden Purchase." *Ariz W*, III(1961):245–264.

19 SCROGGS, William O. *Filibusters and Financiers: The Story of William Walker and His Associates*. New York, 1916.

20 STEVANS, Sylvester K. *American Expansionism in Hawaii, 1842–1898*. Harrisburg, Pa., 1945.

21 TATE, Merze. "Slavery and Racism as Deterrents to the Annexation of Hawaii, 1854–1855." *J Neg Hist*, XLVII(1962):1–18.

22 URBAN, C. Stanley. "The Abortive Quitman Filibustering Expedition, 1853–1855." *J Miss Hist*, XVIII(1956), 175–196.

1   WALLACE, Edward S. *Destiny and Glory*. New York, 1957. (Filibustering.)

2   WARNER, Donald F. *The Idea of Continental Union: Agitation for the Annexation of Canada to the United States, 1849–1893*. Lexington, Ky., 1960.

16. Biography
(Listed alphabetically by subject.)

3   BONSALL, Stephen. *Edward Fitzgerald Beale, a Pioneer in the Path of Empire, 1822–1903*. New York, 1912.

4   ALTER, J. Cecil. *James Bridger, Trapper, Frontiersman, Scout and Guide* Salt Lake City, 1925.

5   VESTAL, Stanley. *Jim Bridger, Mountain Man*. New York, 1946.

6   ESTERGREEN, M. Morgan. *Kit Carson: A Portrait in Courage*. Norman. Okla., 1962.

7   SABIN, Edwin L. *Kit Carson Days, 1809–1868*. Rev. ed. 2 vols. New York, 1935. (First published in 1914.)

8   SCHERER, James A. B. *The Lion of the Vigilantes: William T. Coleman and the Life of Old San Francisco*. Indianapolis, 1939.

9   YOUNG, Otis E. *The West of Philip St. George Cooke, 1809–1895*. Glendale, Calif., 1955.

10   SMITH, Alice Elizabeth. *James Duane Doty, Frontier Promoter*. Madison, Wis., 1950.

11   HAFEN, LeRoy R., and W. J. GHENT. *Broken-Hand: The Life Story of Thomas Fitzpatrick*. Denver, 1931.

12   NEVINS, Allan. *Frémont, Pathmarker of the West*. Rev. ed. New York, 1955. (Published in 1939, the first edition was itself a revision of an earlier and more laudatory book with a different title, published in 1928.)

13   LEWIS, Lloyd. *Captain Sam Grant*. Boston, 1950.

14   DU BOIS, James T., and Gertrude S. MATHEWS. *Galusha A. Grow, Father of the Homestead Law*. Boston, 1917.

15   BAILEY, Paul. *Jacob Hamblin, Buckskin Apostle*. Los Angeles, 1961.

16   FRIEND, Llerena. *Sam Houston, the Great Designer*. Austin, 1954.

17   JAMES, Marquis. *The Raven: A Biography of Sam Houston*. Indianapolis, 1929.†

18   WISEHART, M. K. *Sam Houston, American Giant*. Washington, 1962.

19   ROLAND, Charles P. *Albert Sidney Johnston, Soldier of Three Republics*. Austin, 1964.

20   GAMBRELL, Herbert Pickens. *Anson Jones, the Last President of Texas*. Garden City, N.Y., 1948.

21   CLARKE, Dwight L. *Stephen Watts Kearny, Soldier of the West*. Norman, Okla., 1961.

1   UNDERHILL, Reuben L. *From Cowhides to Golden Fleece: A Narrative of California, 1832–1858.* Stanford, 1939. (Biography of Thomas Oliver Larkin.)

2   HOLMAN, Frederick V. *Dr John McLoughlin, the Father of Oregon.* Cleveland, 1907.

3   STONEHOUSE, Merlin. *John Wesley North and the Reform Frontier.* Minneapolis, 1965.

4   SELLERS, Charles G. *James K. Polk, Continentalist: 1843–1848.* Princeton, 1966.

5   *Memoirs of Lieut.-General Scott, LL.D., Written by Himself.* 2 vols. New York, 1864. (Extends through Mexican War.)

6   ELLIOTT, Charles W. *Winfield Scott, the Soldier and the Man.* New York, 1937.

7   BRODIE, Fawn M. *No Man Knows My History: The Life of Joseph Smith, the Mormon Prophet.* New York, 1945.

8   MOORE, J. Preston. "Pierre Soulé, Southern Expansionist and Promoter." *J S Hist*, XXI(1955):203–223.

9   ZOLLINGER, James Peter. *Sutter, the Man and His Empire.* New York, 1939.

10 DYER, Brainerd. *Zachary Taylor.* Baton Rouge, 1946.

11 HAMILTON, Holman. *Zachary Taylor, Soldier of the Republic.* Indianapolis, 1941.

12 JORDAN, H. Donaldson. "A Politician of Expansion: Robert J. Walker." *Miss Val Hist Rev*, XIX(1932):362–381.

13 FAVOUR, Alpheus H. *Old Bill Williams, Mountain Man.* Chapel Hill, N.C., 1936.

14 WERNER, M. R. *Brigham Young.* New York, 1925.

III. Government and Politics

1. Bibliography and Historiography

15 ALEXANDER, Thomas B. "Historical Treatments of the Dred Scott Case." *Proc N C Hist Assn*, 1953, 37–60.

16 ALLIS, Frederick S., Jr. "The Dred Scott Labyrinth." *Teachers of History.* Ed. by H. Stuart Hughes. Ithaca, N.Y., 1954.

17 BAILEY, Thomas A. *A Diplomatic History of the American People.* 7th ed. New York, 1964. (Critical end-chapter and supplementary bibliographies; particularly, Chapters 15–21.)

18 BEMIS, Samuel Flagg, and Gràce Gardner GRIFFIN. *Guide to the Diplomatic History of the United States, 1775–1921.* Washington, 1935.

19 HORN, James J. "Trends in Historical Interpretation: James K. Polk." *N C Hist Rev*, XLII(1965):454–464.

1 TRASK, David F., Michael C. MEYER, and Roger P. TRASK. *A Bibliography of United States–Latin American Relations since 1810.* Lincoln, Neb., 1968.

2. Selected Source Materials

2 BROOKS, Robert P., and Chauncey S. BOUCHER, eds. *Correspondence Addressed to John C. Calhoun, 1837–1849. Ann Rep Am Hist Assn, 1929,* 125–533.

3 BURNHAM, W. Dean. *Presidential Ballots, 1836–1892.* Baltimore, 1955.

4 HENDERSON, C. B., ed. "Southern Designs on Cuba, 1854–1857, and Some European Opinions." *J S Hist,* V(1939):371–385. (Mainly British documents.)

5 MANNING, William R., ed. *Diplomatic Correspondence of the United States: Canadian Relations, 1784–1860.* 4 vols. Washington, 1940–1945.

6 MANNING, William R., ed. *Diplomatic Correspondence of the United States: Inter-American Affairs, 1831–1860.* 12 vols. Washington, 1932–1939.

7 MILLER, [David] Hunter, ed. *Treaties and Other International Acts of the United States.* 8 vols. Washington, 1931–1948.

8 PETERSEN, Svend. *A Statistical History of the American Presidential Elections.* New York, 1963.

9 PORTER, Kirk H., and Donald Bruce JOHNSON, eds. *National Party Platforms, 1840–1956.* Urbana, Ill., 1956.†

10 PREBLE, George Henry. *The Opening of Japan: A Diary of Discovery in the Far East, 1853–1856.* Ed. by Boleslaw Szczesniak. Norman, Okla., 1962.

11 QUAIFE, Milo Milton, ed. *The Diary of James K. Polk.* See 10.1.

12 SILBEY, Joel H., ed. *The Transformation of American Politics, 1840–1860.* Englewood Cliffs, N.J., 1967.†

13 SMITH, James Morton, and Paul L. MURPHY, eds. *Liberty and Justice: A Historical Record of American Constitutional Development.* New York, 1958.†

14 SWISHER, Earl. *China's Management of the American Barbarians: A Study of Sino-American Relations, 1841–1861, with Documents.* New Haven, Conn., 1953.

3. Constitutional and Legal History

15 AUMANN, Francis R. *The Changing American Legal System: Some Selected Phases.* Columbus, Ohio, 1940.

16 BAUER, Elizabeth K. *Commentaries on the Constitution, 1790–1860.* New York, 1952.

17 BESTOR, Arthur. "The American Civil War as a Constitutional Crisis". *Am Hist Rev,* XLIX(1964):327–352.

1 BURKE, Joseph C. "What Did the Prigg Decision Really Decide?" *Pa Mag*, XCIII(1969):73–85.

2 CORWIN, Edward S. "The Doctrine of Due Process of Law before the Civil War." *Har Law Rev*, XXIV(1911):366–385; 460–479.

3 DENNISON, George Marshel. "The Constitutional Issues of the Dorr War: A Study in the Evolution of American Constitutionalism, 1776–1849." Doctoral dissertation, University of Washington, 1967.

4 DODD, Walter Fairleigh. *The Revision and Amendment of State Constitutions.* Baltimore, 1910.

5 ELAZAR, Daniel J. *The American Partnership: Intergovernmental Co-operation in the Nineteenth-Century United States.* Chicago, 1962.

6 GREEN, Fletcher M. *Constitutional Development in the South Atlantic States, 1776–1860.* Chapel Hill, N.C., 1930.†

7 HAINES, Charles Grove, and Foster H. SHERWOOD. *The Role of the Supreme Court in American Government and Politics, 1835–1864.* Berkeley, 1957.

8 HOCKETT, Homer Carey. *The Constitutional History of the United States.* 2 vols. New York, 1939. (Vol. II: 1826–1876.)

9 HOPKINS, Vincent C. *Dred Scott's Case.* New York, 1951.†

10 KELLY, Alfred H., and Winfred A. HARBISON. *The American Constitution: Its Origins and Development.* 3rd ed. New York, 1963.

11 KUTLER, Stanley I., ed. *The Dred Scott Decision: Law or Politics?* Boston, 1967.† (Sources and scholarly essays with useful introduction.)

12 LESLIE, William R. "The Influence of Joseph Story's Theory of the Conflict of Laws on Constitutional Nationalism." *Miss Val Hist Rev*, XXXV(1948): 203–220.

13 MC LAUGHLIN, Andrew C. *A Constitutional History of the United States.* New York, 1935.

14 MENDELSOHN, Wallace. "Chief Justice Taney, Jacksonian Judge." *Pitt Law Rev*, XII(1951):381–393.

15 MILLER, Perry. *The Life of the Mind in America, from the Revolution to the Civil War.* New York, 1965. (Development of law treated extensively.)

16 SCHMIDHAUSER, John R. "Judicial Behavior and the Sectional Crisis of 1837–1860." *J Pol*, XXIII(1961):615–640.

17 SCHMIDHAUSER, John R. *The Supreme Court as Final Arbiter in Federal-State Relations, 1789–1957.* Chapel Hill, N.C., 1958.

18 STILL, Bayrd. "An Interpretation of the Statehood Process, 1800 to 1850." *Miss Val Hist Rev*, XXIII(1936), 189–204. (Compares state constitutions.)

19 WARREN, Charles. *A History of the American Bar.* Boston, 1911.

20 WARREN, Charles. *The Supreme Court in United States History.* 3 vols. Boston, 1922. (Later editions are 2 vols.)

4. Congress and the Presidency

1 ALEXANDER, Thomas B. *Sectional Stress and Party Strength: A Study of Roll-Call Voting Patterns in the United States House of Representatives, 1836–1860*. Nashville, 1967. (Largely statistical, an immense amount of information.)

2 BAILEY, Thomas A. *Presidential Greatness: The Image and the Man from George Washington to the Present*. New York, 1966.†

3 BINKLEY, Wilfred E. *President and Congress*. New York, 1947.†

4 BOYAKIN, Edward. *Congress and the Civil War*. New York, 1955.

5 EBERLING, Ernest J. *Congressional Investigations*. New York, 1928.

6 GRAEBNER, Norman A. "James K. Polk: A Study in Federal Patronage." *Miss Val Hist Rev*, XXXVIII(1952):613–632.

7 HART, Charles Desmond. "Congressmen and the Expansion of Slavery into the Territories: A Study in Attitudes, 1846–1861." Doctoral dissertation, University of Washington, 1965.

8 JACKSON, Carlton. *Presidential Vetoes, 1792–1945*. Athens, Ga., 1967. (Extensive treatment of 1841–1861.)

9 LAMBERT, Oscar Doane. *Presidential Politics in the United States, 1841–1844*. Durham, N.C., 1936.

10 LEVIN, Peter R. *Seven by Chance: The Accidental Presidents*. New York, 1948. (Tyler and Fillmore.)

11 MC COY, Charles A. *Polk and the Presidency*. Austin, 1960. (Studies the President in each of his major roles.)

12 MORGAN, Robert J. *A Whig Embattled: The Presidency under John Tyler*. Lincoln, Neb., 1954.

13 SILBEY, Joel H. "John C. Calhoun and the Limits of Southern Congressional Unity, 1841–1850." *Historian*, XXX(1967):58–71.

14 SILBEY, Joel H. *The Shrine of Party: Congressional Voting Behavior, 1841–1852*. Pittsburgh, 1967.

15 SUTHERLAND, Keith Alan. "Congress and Crisis: A Study in the Legislative Process, 1860." Doctoral dissertation, Cornell University, 1966.

16 YARWOOD, Dean L. "Legislative Persistence: A Comparison of the United States Senate in 1850 and 1860." *Midw J Pol Sci*, XI(1967):193–211.

5. The Administration of Government

17 BARNES, Harry Elmer. *The Evolution of Penology in Pennsylvania*. Indianapolis, 1927.

18 BLAKE, Nelson M. *Water for the Cities: A History of the Urban Water-Supply Problem in the United States*. Syracuse, 1956. (Four eastern cities, 1790–1860.)

1　CLARK, John B., Jr. "Fire Protection in the Old South." 2 vols. Doctoral dissertation, University of Kentucky, 1957.

2　FEHRENBACHER, Don E. "The Post Office in Illinois Politics of the 1850's." *J Ill St Hist Soc*, XLVI(1953):60–70.

3　FISH, Carl Russell. *The Civil Service and the Patronage*. New York, 1905.

4　FOWLER, Dorothy Ganfield. *The Cabinet Politician: The Postmasters General, 1829–1909*. New York, 1943.

5　HARLOW, Alvin F. *Old Post Bags: The Story of the Sending of a Letter in Ancient and Modern Times*. New York, 1928.

6　LANE, Roger. *Policing the City: Boston, 1822–1885*. Cambridge, Mass., 1967.

7　LEWIS, W. David. *From Newgate to Dannemora: The Rise of the Penitentiary in New York, 1796–1848*. Ithaca, N.Y., 1965. (The author's doctoral dissertation, Cornell University, 1961, carries the study to 1861.)

8　MC KELVEY, Blake. *American Prisons: A Study in American Social History Prior to 1915*. Chicago, 1936.

9　NEILLY, Andrew H. "The Violent Volunteers: A History of the Volunteer Fire Department of Philadelphia, 1736–1871." Doctoral dissertation, University of Pennsylvania, 1966.

10　RICHARDSON, James F. "The History of Police Protection in New York City, 1800–1870." Doctoral dissertation, New York University, 1961.

11　SHORT, Lloyd Milton. *The Development of National Administrative Organization in the United States*. Baltimore, 1923.

12　STUART, Graham H. *The Department of State: A History of Its Organization, Procedure, and Personnel*. New York, 1949.

13　WHITE, Leonard D. *The Jacksonians: A Study in Administrative History, 1829–1861*. New York, 1954.†

14　WILLIAMS, Jack K. *Vogues in Villainy: Crime and Retribution in Ante-Bellum South Carolina*. Columbia, S.C., 1959.

6. *Foreign Relations*

15　BAILEY, Thomas A. *A Diplomatic History*. See 25.17.

16　BEMIS, Samuel Flagg, ed. *The American Secretaries of State and Their Diplomacy*. 10 vols. New York, 1927–1929. (Particularly, Vols. V and VI.)

17　BEMIS, Samuel Flagg. *A Diplomatic History of the United States*. 5th ed. New York, 1965.

18　BLUMENTHAL, Henry. *A Reappraisal of Franco-American Relations, 1830–1871*. Chapel Hill, N.C., 1959.

19　BOURNE, Kenneth. *Britain and the Balance of Power in North America, 1815–1908*. Berkeley, 1967.

1 CALLAHAN, James Morton. *American Foreign Policy in Canadian Relations*. New York, 1937.

2 CALLAHAN, James Morton. *American Foreign Policy in Mexican Relations*. New York, 1932,

3 COREY, Albert B. *The Crisis of 1830–1842 in Canadian-American Relations*. New Haven, Conn., 1941. (Background of Webster-Ashburton Treaty.)

4 DULLES, Foster Rhea. *Yankees and Samurai: America's Role in the Emergence of Modern Japan, 1791–1900*. New York, 1965.

5 ETTINGER, Amos Aschbach. *The Mission to Spain of Pierre Soulé, 1853–1855*. New Haven, Conn., 1932.

6 FONER, Philip S. *A History of Cuba*. See 23.14.

7 GRIFFIN, Eldon. *Clippers and Consuls: American Consular and Commercial Relations with Eastern Asia, 1845–1860*. Ann Arbor, Mich., 1938.

8 JONES, Wilbur D. *Lord Aberdeen and the Americas*. See 20.10.

9 LANDRY, Harral E. "Slavery and the Slave Trade in Atlantic Diplomacy, 1850–1861." *J S Hist*, XXVII(1961):184–207.

10 LILLIBRIDGE, George D. *Beacon of Freedom: The Impact of American Democracy upon Great Britain, 1830–1870*. Philadelphia, 1954.†

11 MAY, Arthur James. *Contemporary American Opinion of the Mid-Century Revolutions in Central Europe*. Philadelphia, 1927.

12 MERK, Frederick. *The Oregon Question*. See 20.15.

13 PERKINS, Dexter. *The Monroe Doctrine, 1826–1867*. Baltimore, 1933.†

14 REEVES, Jesse S. *American Diplomacy under Tyler and Polk*. See 19.8.

15 RIVES, George L. *The United States and Mexico*. See 19.9.

16 SHARROW, Walter G. "William Henry Seward and the Basis for American Empire, 1850–1860." *Pac Hist Rev*, XXXVI(1967):325–342.

17 SHIPPEE, Lester Burrell. *Canadian-American Relations, 1849–1874*. New Haven, Conn., 1939.

18 SOULSBY, Hugh G. *The Right of Search and the Slave Trade in Anglo-American Relations, 1814–1862*. *Stud Hist Pol Sci* (Hop), LI. Baltimore, 1933.

19 SPENCER, Donald S. "Lewis Cass and Symbolic Intervention: 1848–1852." *Mich Hist*, LIII(1969):1–17.

20 TONG, Te-kong. *United States Diplomacy in China, 1844–60*. Seattle, 1964.

21 TREAT, Payson Jackson. *The Early Diplomatic Relations between the United States and Japan, 1853–1865*. Baltimore, 1917.

22 WALWORTH, Arthur C. *Black Ships off Japan: The Story of Commodore Perry's Expedition*. New York, 1946.

23 WILLIAMS, Mary Wilhelmine. *Anglo-American Isthmian Diplomacy, 1815–1915*. Washington, 1916. (Extensive treatment of 1850's.)

7. *Political Parties and Elections*

A. General

1 BENTON, Thomas Hart. *Thirty Years View.* 2 vols. New York, 1854–1856.

2 BINKLEY, Wilfred E. *American Political Parties: Their Natural History.* 4th ed. New York, 1962.

3 HOFSTADTER, Richard. *The American Political Tradition and the Men Who Made It.* New York, 1948.†

4 NICHOLS, Roy F. *The Invention of the American Political Parties.* New York, 1967.

5 ROSEBOOM, Eugene H. *A History of Presidential Elections.* New York, 1957.

6 WILLIAMSON, Chilton. *American Suffrage: From Property to Democracy, 1760–1860.* Princeton, 1960.†

B. Specific Parties

7 BLUE, Frederick Judd. "A History of the Free Soil Party." Doctoral dissertation, University of Wisconsin, 1966.

8 BROUSSARD, James H. "Some Determinants of Know-Nothing Electoral Strength in the South, 1856." *La Hist*, VII(1966):5–20.

9 COLE, Arthur Charles. *The Whig Party in the South.* Washington, 1913.

10 CRANDALL, Andrew W. *The Early History' of the Republican Party, 1854–1856.* Boston, 1930.

11 FONER, Eric. "Politics and Prejudice: The Free Soil Party and the Negro, 1849–1852." *J Neg Hist*, L(1965):239–256.

12 HAMILTON, Charles Granville. *Lincoln and the Know Nothing Movement.* Washington, 1954. (Pamphlet.)

13 LYNCH, William O. "Anti-Slavery Tendencies of the Democratic Party in the Northwest, 1848–1850." *Miss Val Hist Rev*, XI(1924):319–331.

14 MAYER, George H. *The Republican Party, 1854–1964.* New York, 1964.†

15 MOOS, Malcolm C. *The Republicans: A History of Their Party.* New York, 1956.

16 NICHOLS, Roy F. *The Democratic Machine, 1850–54.* New York, 1923.

17 OVERDYKE, W. Darrell. *The Know-Nothing Party in the South.* Baton Rouge, 1950.

18 PARKS, Gordon Elliott. "Martin Van Buren and the Re-organization of the Democratic Party, 1841–1844." Doctoral dissertation, University of Wisconsin, 1965.

1   PAUL, James C. N. *Rift in the Democracy*. Philadelphia, 1951.† (1840–1844.)

.2   SILBEY, Joel H. "The Southern National Democrats, 1845–1861." *Mid-Am*, XLVII(1965):176–190.

3   SMITH, Theodore Clarke. *The Liberty and Free Soil Parties in the Northwest*. New York, 1897.

C. Specific Elections

4   BARTLETT, Ruhl J. *John C. Frémont and the Republican Party*. Columbus, Ohio, 1930. (Election of 1856.)

5   CRENSHAW, Ollinger. *The Slave States in the Presidential Election of 1860*. *Stud Hist Pol Sci* (Hop), LXIII. Baltimore, 1945.

6   FITE, Emerson David. *The Presidential Campaign of 1860*. New York, 1911.

7   GRAEBNER, Norman A., ed. *Politics and the Crisis of 1860*. Urbana, Ill., 1961. (Essays by five historians.)

8   GRAEBNER, Norman A. "Thomas Corwin and the Election of 1848: A Study in Conservative Politics." *J S Hist*, XVII(1951):162–179.

9   GUNDERSON, Robert Gray. *The Log Cabin Campaign*. Lexington, Ky., 1957. (Election of 1840.)

10   LUTHIN, Reinhard H. *The First Lincoln Campaign*. Cambridge, Mass., 1944.

11   MEERSE, David E. "Buchanan, Corruption, and the Election of 1860." *Civ War Hist*, XII(1966):116–131.

12   MILES, Edwin A. "Fifty-Four Forty or Fight." See 18.8.

13   PITKIN, Thomas M. "Western Republicans and the Tariff in 1860." *Miss Val Hist Rev*, XXVII(1940):401–420.

14   WYNNE, Patricia Hochwalt. "Lincoln's Western Image in the 1860 Campaign." *Md Hist Mag*, LIX(1964):165–181.

8. State and Local Politics
(Listed geographically by states)

15   WESCOTT, Richard Rollins. "A History of Maine Politics, 1840–1856: The Formation of the Republican Party." Doctoral dissertation, University of Maine, 1966.

16   BEAN, William G. "Puritan versus Celt, 1850–1860." *N Eng Q*, VII(1934): 70–89. (Massachusetts.)

17   DARLING, Arthur B. *Political Changes in Massachusetts, 1824–1848*. New Haven, Conn., 1925.

18   GATELL, Frank Otto. " 'Conscience and Judgment': The Bolt of the Massachusetts Conscience Whigs." *Historian*, XXI(1958):18–45.

19   MULKERN, John Raymond. "The Know-Nothing Party in Massachusetts." Doctoral dissertation, Boston University, 1963.

1   PARMET, Robert David. "The Know-Nothings in Connecticut." Doctoral dissertation, Columbia University, 1966.

2   ALEXANDER, DeAlva S. *A Political History of the State of New York.* 3 vols. New York, 1906–1909. (Particularly, Vol. II.)

3   BENSON, Lee. *The Concept of Jacksonian Democracy: New York as a Test Case.* Princeton, 1961.†

4   CARMAN, Harry J., and Reinhard H. LUTHIN. "The Seward-Fillmore Feud and the Disruption of the Whig Party." *N Y Hist,* XXIV(1943):335–357.

5   CHALMERS, Leonard. "Tammany Hall and New York City Politics, 1853–1861." Doctoral dissertation, New York University, 1967.

6   CURRAN, Thomas J. "Know Nothings of New York." Doctoral dissertation, Columbia University, 1963.

7   CURRAN, Thomas J. "Seward and the Know-Nothings." *N Y Hist Soc Q,* LI(1967):141–159.

8   DONOVAN, Herbert D. A. *The Barnburners.* New York, 1925. (New York politics, 1830–1852.)

9   FERREE, Walter L. "The New York Democracy: Division and Reunion, 1847–1852." Doctoral dissertation, University of Pennsylvania, 1953.

10 LEONARD, Ira M. "New York City Politics, 1841–1844: Nativism and Reform." Doctoral dissertation, New York University, 1965.

11 LEONARD, Ira M. "The Rise and Fall of the American Republican Party in New York City, 1843–1845." *N Y Hist Soc Q,* L(1966):151–192.

12 LONDON, Herbert Ira. "The Nativist Movement in the American Republican Party in New York City During the Period 1843–1847." Doctoral dissertation, New York University, 1966.

13 SCISCO, Louis Dow. *Political Nativism in New York. Stud Hist Econ Pub Law* (Colum), XIII. New York, 1901.

14 WERNER, M. R. *Tammany Hall.* Garden City, N.Y., 1928.

15 HOLT, Michael Fitzgibbon. *Forging a Majority: The Formation of the Republican Party in Pittsburgh, 1848–1860.* New Haven, Conn., 1969.

16 KLEPPNER, Paul J. "Lincoln and the Immigrant Vote: A Case of Religious Polarization." *Mid-Am,* XLVIII(1965):176–195. (Pittsburgh.)

17 MUELLER, Henry R. *The Whig Party in Pennsylvania.* New York, 1922.

18 MC CONVILLE, Mary St. Patrick. *Political Nativism in the State of Maryland, 1830–1860.* Washington, 1928.

19 SCHMECKEBIER, Laurence F. *The History of the Know Nothing Party in Maryland. Stud Hist Pol Sci* (Hop), XVII. Baltimore, 1899.

20 SMITH, Wilbur Wayne. "The Whig Party in Maryland, 1826–1856." Doctoral dissertation, University of Maryland, 1967.

21 EATON, Clement. "Henry A. Wise and the Virginia Fire Eaters of 1856." *Miss Val Hist Rev,* XXI(1935):495–512.

1 RICE, Philip Morrison. "The Know-Nothing Party in Virginia, 1854–1856." *Va Mag Hist Biog*, LV(1947):61–75, 159–167.

2 MORRILL, James R. "The Presidential Election of 1852, Death Knell of the Whig Party of North Carolina." *N C Hist Rev*, XLIV(1967):342–359.

3 NORTON, Clarence Clifford. *The Democratic Party in Ante-Bellum North Carolina, 1835–1861.* Chapel Hill, N.C., 1930.

4 MONTGOMERY, Horace. *Cracker Parties.* Baton Rouge, 1950. (Georgia.)

5 DOHERTY, Herbert J., Jr. *The Whigs of Florida, 1845–1854.* Gainesville, Fla., 1959.

6 ALEXANDER, Thomas B., et al. "The Basis of Alabama's Ante-Bellum Two-Party System." *Ala Rev*, XIX(1966):243–277.

7 ALEXANDER, Thomas B., et al. "Who Were the Alabama Whigs?" *Ala Rev*, XVI(1963):5–19.

8 JACKSON, Carlton. "A History of the Whig Party in Alabama, 1828–1860." Doctoral dissertation, University of Alabama, 1963.

9 JONES, Allan W. "Party Nominating Machinery in Ante-Bellum Alabama." *Ala Rev*, XX(1967):34–44.

10 MC WHINEY, Grady. "Were the Whigs a Class Party in Alabama?" *J S Hist*, XXIII(1957):510–522.

11 RAWSON, Donald M. "Party Politics in Mississippi, 1850–1860." Doctoral dissertation, Vanderbilt University, 1964.

12 ADAMS, William Harrison, III. "The Louisiana Whig Party." Doctora dissertation, Louisiana State University, 1960.

13 SOULÉ, Leon Cyprian. *The Know-Nothing Party in New Orleans.* Baton Rouge, 1961.

14 BERGERON, Paul Herbert. "The Jacksonian Party on Trial: Presidential Politics in Tennessee, 1836–1856." Doctoral dissertation, Vanderbilt University, 1965.

15 TRICAMO, John Edgar. "Tennessee Politics, 1845–1861." Doctoral dissertation, Columbia University, 1965.

16 MC GANN, Agnes Geraldine. *Nativism in Kentucky to 1860.* Washington, 1944.

17 MERING, John Vollmer. *The Whig Party in Missouri.* Columbia, Mo., 1967.

18 BLUE, Frederick Judd. "The Ohio Free Soilers and Problems of Factionalism." *Ohio Hist*, LXXVII(1967):17–32, 89–93.

19 HOLT, Edgar Allan. "Party Politics in Ohio, 1840–1850." *Ohio Arch Hist Pub*, XXXVII(1928):439–591; XXXVIII(1929):47–182, 260–402. (Serialized doctoral dissertation.)

20 RAYBACK, Joseph. "The Liberty Party Leaders of Ohio: Exponents of Antislavery Coalition." *Ohio St Arch Hist Q*, LVII(1948):165–178.

21 SIMMS, Henry H. *Ohio Politics on the Eve of Conflict.* Columbus, Ohio, 1961. (Pamphlet.)

1 BRAND, Carl Fremont. "History of the Know Nothing Party in Indiana." *Ind Mag Hist*, XVIII(1922):47–81, 177–206, 266–306.

2 ELBERT, Elmer Duane. "Southern Indiana Politics on the Eve of the Civil War, 1858–1861." Doctoral dissertation, University of Indiana, 1967.

3 VAN BOLT, Roger A. "Sectional Aspects of Expansion, 1844–1848." *Ind Mag Hist*, XLVIII(1952):119–140. (Indiana politics.)

4 ZIMMERMAN, Charles. "The Origin and Rise of the Republican Party in Indiana from 1854 to 1860." *Ind Mag Hist*, XIII(1917):211–269, 349–412.

5 BARINGER, William E. "Campaign Technique in Illinois—1860." *Tran Ill St Hist Soc*, No. 39(1932):203–281.

6 BERGQUIST, James Manning. "The Political Attitudes of the German Immigrant in Illinois, 1848–1860." Doctoral dissertation, Northwestern University, 1966.

7 SENNING, John P. "The Know-Nothing Movement in Illinois, 1854–1856." *J Ill St Hist Soc*, VII(1914):7–33.

8 FORMISANO, Ronald Paul. "The Social Bases of American Voting Behavior: Wayne County, Michigan, 1837–1852, as a Test Case." Doctoral dissertation, Wayne State University, 1966.

9 STREETER, Floyd Benjamin. *Political Parties in Michigan, 1837–1860*. Lansing, Mich., 1918.

10 SCHAFER, Joseph. "Know-Nothingism in Wisconsin." *Wis Mag Hist*, VIII(1924):3–21.

11 DANIELS, George H. "Immigrant Vote in the 1860 Election: The Case of Iowa." *Mid-Am*, XLIV(1962):146–162.

12 ROSENBERG, Morton M. "The Democratic Party of Iowa, 1850–1860." Doctoral dissertation, University of Iowa, 1957.

13 SPARKS, David S. "The Birth of the Republican Party in Iowa, 1854–1856." *Iowa J Hist*, LIV(1956):1–34.

14 SWIERENGA, Robert P. "The Ethnic Voter and the First Lincoln Election." *Civ War Hist*, XI(1965):27–43. (Iowa.)

15 CAMPBELL, Randolph. "The Whig Party of Texas in the Elections of 1848 and 1852." *SW Hist Q*, LXXIII(1969):17–34.

16 WOOSTER, Ralph A. "An Analysis of the Texas Know-Nothings." *SW Hist Q*, LXX(1967):414–423.

17 HURT, Peyton. "The Rise and Fall of the Know Nothings in California." *Calif Hist Soc Q*, IX(1930):16–49, 100–128.

18 POMEROY, Earl. "California, 1846–1860: Politics of a Representative Frontier State." *Calif Hist Soc Q*, XXXII(1953):291–302.

19 HENDRICKSON, James E. "The Rupture of the Democratic Party in Oregon, 1858." *Pac NW Q*, LVIII(1967):65–73.

20 JOHANNSEN, Robert W. *Frontier Politics and the Sectional Conflict: The Pacific Northwest on the Eve of the Civil War*. Seattle, 1955.† (Paperback edition has variant title.)

9. *Biography*

(Listed alphabetically by subject; for political biography, see also 96.19–102.11.)

21 BEMIS, Samuel Flagg. *John Quincy Adams and the Union*. New York, 1956.

1   NYE, Russel B. *George Bancroft, Brahmin Rebel.* New York, 1944.†

2   CHAMBERS, William Nisbet. *Old Bullion Benton, Senator from the New West: Thomas Hart Benton, 1782–1858.* Boston, 1956.

3   SMITH, Elbert B. *Magnificent Missourian: The Life of Thomas Hart Benton.* Philadelphia, 1958.

4   SMITH, William Ernest. *The Francis Preston Blair Family in Politics.* 2 vols. New York, 1933.

5   CAPERS, Gerald M. *John C. Calhoun, Opportunist: A Reappraisal.* Gainesville, Fla., 1960.

6   COIT, Margaret L. *John C. Calhoun: American Portrait.* Boston, 1950.†

7   FITZSIMONS, Matthew A. "Calhoun's Bid for the Presidency, 1841–1844." *Miss Val Hist Rev,* XXXVIII(1951):39–60.

8   RAYBACK, Joseph. "The Presidential Ambitions of John C. Calhoun, 1844–1848." *J S Hist,* XIV(1948):331–356.

9   THOMAS, John L., ed. *John C. Calhoun: A Profile.* New York, 1968.† (Anthology of essays.)

10 WILTSE, Charles M. *John C. Calhoun, Sectionalist, 1840–1850.* Indianapolis, 1951. (Part of a 3-volume biography, the fullest available.)

11 MC LAUGHLIN, Andrew C. *Lewis Cass.* Boston, 1891.

12 WOODFORD, Frank B. *Lewis Cass, the Last Jeffersonian.* New Brunswick, N.J., 1950.

13 EATON, Clement. *Henry Clay and the Art of American Politics.* Boston, 1957.†

14 POAGE, George Rawlings. *Henry Clay and the Whig Party.* Chapel Hill, N.C., 1936.

15 VAN DEUSEN, Glyndon G. *The Life of Henry Clay.* Boston, 1937.†

16 COHEN, Henry. "Business and Politics from the Age of Jackson to the Civil War: A Study from the Life of W. W. Corcoran." Doctoral dissertation Cornell University, 1965.

17 LEACH, Richard H. "Benjamin Robbins Curtis: Judicial Misfit." *N Eng Q,* XXV(1952):507–523.

18 FRANK, John P. *Justice Daniel Dissenting: A Biography of Peter V. Daniel, 1784–1860.* Cambridge, Mass., 1964.

19 DIX, Morgan, comp. *Memoirs of John Adams Dix.* 2 vols. New York, 1883.

20 FROTHINGHAM, Paul Revere. *Edward Everett, Orator and Statesman.* Boston, 1925.

21 CROW, Carl. *He Opened the Door of Japan: Townsend Harris and the Story of His Amazing Adventures in Establishing American Relations with the Far East.* New York, 1939.

22 MEIGS, William M. *The Life of Charles Jared Ingersoll.* Philadelphia, 1897.

23 STEINER, Bernard C. *Life of Reverdy Johnson.* Baltimore, 1914.

1   STEEL, Edward M., Jr. *T. Butler King of Georgia.* Athens, Ga., 1964.

2   RIDDLE, Donald W. *Congressman Abraham Lincoln.* Urbana, Ill., 1957.

3   WEISENBURGER, Francis P. *The Life of John McLean, a Politician on the United States Supreme Court.* Columbus, Ohio, 1937.

4   SPENCER, Ivor Debenham. *The Victor and the Spoils: A Life of William L. Marcy.* Providence, 1959.

5   LOWENTHAL, David. *George Perkins Marsh, Versatile Vermonter.* New York, 1958.

6   BARROWS, Edward M. *The Great Commodore: The Exploits of Matthew Calbraith Perry.* Indianapolis, 1935.

7   MORISON, Samuel Eliot. *"Old Bruin," Commodore Matthew C. Perry, 1794–1858.* Boston, 1967.

8   GRAEBNER, Norman A. "James Polk." *America's Ten Greatest Presidents.* Ed. by Morton Borden. Chicago, 1961.†

9   MCCORMAC, Eugene I. *James K. Polk: A Political Biography.* Berkeley, 1922.

10 SELLERS, Charles G. *James K. Polk: Jacksonian, 1795–1843;* and *James K. Polk: Continentalist, 1843–1848.* Princeton, 1957, 1966.

11 LEVY, Leonard W. *The Law of the Commonwealth and Chief Justice Shaw.* Cambridge, Mass., 1957.

12 HARRIS, Robert J. "Chief Justice Taney, Prophet of Reform and Reaction." *American Constitutional Law, Historical Essays.* Ed. by Leonard W. Levy. New York, 1966.†

13 LEWIS, Walker. *Without Fear or Favor: A Biography of Chief Justice Roger Brooke Taney.* Boston, 1965.

14 SMITH, Charles W., Jr. *Roger B. Taney, Jacksonian Jurist.* Chapel Hill, N.C., 1936.

15 SWISHER, Carl Brent. *Roger B. Taney.* New York, 1935. (The fullest treatment.)

16 CHITWOOD, Oliver Perry. *John Tyler, Champion of the Old South.* New York, 1939.

17 SEAGER, Robert, II. *And Tyler Too: A Biography of John and Julia Gardiner Tyler.* New York, 1963.

18 WISE, Henry A. *Seven Decades of the Union.* Philadelphia, 1872. (Life and times of John Tyler.)

19 SHENTON, James P. *Robert John Walker: A Politician from Jackson to Lincoln.* New York, 1961.

20 LAWRENCE, Alexander A. *James Moore Wayne, Southern Unionist.* Chapel Hill, N.C., 1943.

21 CURRENT, Richard N. *Daniel Webster and the Rise of National Conservatism.* Boston, 1955.†

22 FUESS, Claude M. *Daniel Webster.* 2 vols. Boston, 1930.

23 FEHRENBACHER, Don E. *Chicago Giant: A Biography of "Long John" Wentworth.* Madison, Wis., 1957.

1   PLEASANTS, Samuel Augustus. *Fernando Wood of New York*. New York, 1948.

2   GARRATY, John A. *Silas Wright*. New York, 1949.

IV. The American Economy

1. Bibliography and Historiography

3   ENGERMAN, Stanley L. "The Effects of Slavery upon the Southern Economy: A Review of the Recent Debate." *Explor Entrepren Hist* [2nd Ser], IV(1967):71–97.

4   GATES, Paul Wallace. *The Farmer's Age: Agriculture, 1815–1860*. New York, 1960.† (Bibliography, 421–439.)

5   HINDLE, Brooke. *Technology in Early America: Needs and Opportunities for Study*. Chapel Hill, N.C., 1966. (Excellent bibliography extends to 1850.)

6   LARSON, Henrietta M. *Guide to Business History*. Cambridge, Mass., 1948.

7   TAYLOR, George Rogers. *American Economic History before 1860*. New York, 1969.† (Goldentree Bibliography.)

8   TAYLOR, George Rogers. *The Transportation Revolution, 1815–1860*. New York, 1951.† (Bibliography, 399–438.)

9   WOODMAN, Harold D. "The Profitability of Slavery, a Historical Perennial." *J S Hist*, XXIX(1963):303–325.

2. Selected Source Materials

10   CALLENDER, Guy Stevens, ed. *Selections from the Economic History of the United States, 1765–1860*. Boston, 1909.

11   COMMONS, John R., et al., eds. *Documentary History of American Industrial Society*. 10 vols. Cleveland, 1910–1911. (Particularly, Vols. VII and VIII.)

12   DE BOW, J. D. B. *The Industrial Resources, Etc., of the Southern and Western States*. 3 vols. New Orleans, 1852–1853.

13   EASTERBY, J. H., ed. *The South Carolina Rice Plantation as Revealed in the Papers of Robert F.W. Allston*. Chicago, 1945.

14   GOODRICH, Carter, ed. *The Government and the Economy, 1783–1861*. Indianapolis, 1967.†

15   KELLAR, Herbert Anthony, ed. *Solon Robinson, Pioneer and Agriculturalist: Selected Writings*. 2 vols. Indianapolis, 1936.

16   PRESSLY, Thomas J., and William H. SCOFIELD, eds. *Farm Real Estate Values in the United States by Counties, 1850–1959*. Seattle, 1965.

3. General Studies

1 ANDREANO, Ralph L., ed. *New Views on American Economic Development.* Cambridge, Mass., 1965. (Anthology of scholarly essays.)

2 BRUCHEY, Stuart. *The Roots of American Economic Growth, 1607–1861.* New York, 1965.†

3 COCHRAN, Thomas C. "Did the Civil War Retard Industrialization?" *Miss Val Hist Rev*, XLVIII(1961):197–210. (A seminal essay, with much on prewar economic growth.)

4 COCHRAN, Thomas C., and Thomas B. BREWER, eds. *Views of American Economic Growth: The Agricultural Era.* New York, 1966. (Anthology of scholarly essays.)

5 DORFMAN, Joseph. *The Economic Mind in American Civilization, 1606–1865.* 2 vols. New York, 1946.

6 GILCHRIST, David T., and W. David LEWIS, eds. *Economic Change in the Civil War Era.* Greenville, Del., 1965.†

7 KUZNETS, Simon. "National Income Estimates for the United States Prior to 1870." *J Econ Hist*, XII(1952):115–130.

8 LEIMAN, Melvin M. *Jacob N. Cardozo: Economic Thought in the Antebellum South.* New York, 1966.

9 MARTIN, Edgar W. *The Standard of Living in 1860: American Consumption Levels on the Eve of the Civil War.* Chicago, 1942.

10 MARTIN, Robert F. *National Income of the United States, 1799–1938.* New York, 1939.

11 MILLER, Douglas T. *Jacksonian Aristocracy: Class and Democracy in New York, 1830–1860.* New York, 1967.

12 NORTH, Douglass C. *Economic Growth of the United States, 1790–1860.* Englewood Cliffs, N.J., 1961.†

13 NORTH, Douglass C. *Growth and Welfare in the American Past: A New Economic History.* Englewood Cliffs, N.J., 1966.†

14 ROSTOW, Walt W. *The Stages of Economic Growth: A Non-Communist Manifesto.* Cambridge, England, 1960.†

15 RUSSEL, Robert R. *A History of the American Economic System.* New York, 1964.

16 TAYLOR, George Rogers. *The Transportation Revolution.* See 38.8.

17 *Trends in the American Economy in the Nineteenth Century.* National Bureau of Economic Research, *Studies in Income and Wealth*, Vol. XXIV. Princeton, 1960. (Technical papers on income, investment, balance of payments, wage trends, etc.)

18 WILLIAMSON, Harold F., ed. *The Growth of the American Economy.* 2nd ed. New York, 1951.

4. Technology

1 BURLINGAME, Roger. *March of the Iron Men: A Social History of Union through Invention*. New York, 1938.†

2 CALHOUN, Daniel Hovey. *The American Civil Engineer: Origins and Conflicts*. Cambridge, Mass., 1960.

3 CALVERT, Monte A. *The Mechanical Engineer in America, 1830–1910: Professional Cultures in Conflict*. Baltimore, 1967.

4 CARTER, Samuel, III. *Cyrus Field, Man of Two Worlds*. New York, 1968.

5 CONDIT, Carl W. *American Building Art: The Nineteenth Century*. New York, 1960.

6 CUMMINGS, Richard O. *The American Ice Harvests: A Historical Study in Technology, 1800–1918*. Berkeley, 1949.

7 DE CAMP, L. Sprague. *The Heroic Age of American Invention*. Garden City, N.Y., 1961.

8 EDWARDS, William B. *The Story of Colt's Revolver: The Biography of Col. Samuel Colt*. Harrisburg, Pa., 1953.

9 FISHER, Marvin. *Workshops in the Wilderness: The European Response to American Industrialization, 1830–1860*. New York, 1967. (Examines the writings of European visitors about American technology.)

10 HABAKKUK, H. J. *American and British Technology in the 19th Century: The Search for Labour Saving Inventions*. Cambridge, England, 1962.

11 ILES, George. *Leading American Inventors*. New York, 1912.

12 KOUWENHOVEN, John A. *Made in America: The Arts in Modern Civilization*. Garden City, N.Y., 1948.† (Paperback edition has variant title.)

13 KRANZBERG, Melvin, and Carroll W. PURSELL, Jr. *Technology in Western Civilization*. 2 vols. New York, 1967. (Particularly, Vol. I.)

14 MABEE, Carleton. *The American Leonardo: A Life of Samuel F. B. Morse*. New York, 1943.

15 MARX, Leo. *The Machine in the Garden: Technology and the Pastoral Ideal in America*. New York, 1964.†

16 MEIER, Hugo A. "Technology and Democracy, 1800–1860." *Miss Val Hist Rev*, XLIII(1957):618–640.

17 OLIVER, John W. *History of American Technology*. New York, 1956.

18 PURSELL, Carroll W., Jr. "Stationary Steam Engines in America before the Civil War." Doctoral dissertation, University of California, 1962.

19 ROGIN, Leo. *The Introduction of Farm Machinery in Its Relation to the Productivity of Labor in the Agriculture of the United States during the Nineteenth Century*. *Pub Econ* (Berk), IX, Berkeley, 1931.

1 SINGER, Charles, et al., eds. *A History of Technology.* 5 vols. Oxford, England, 1954–1958. (A monumental work that contains much information on, or relevant to, American technology. See particularly Vols. IV and V.)

2 STRASSMAN, W. Paul. *Risk and Technological Innovation: American Manufacturing Methods during the Nineteenth Century.* Ithaca, N.Y., 1959.

3 TEMIN, Peter. "Labor Scarcity and the Problem of American Industrial Efficiency in the 1850's." *J Econ Hist,* XXVI(1966):277–298.

4 WHITE, Ruth. *Yankee from Sweden: The Dream and the Reality in the Days of John Ericsson.* New York, 1960.

5 WOLF, Ralph F. *India Rubber Man: The Story of Charles Goodyear.* Caldwell, Idaho, 1939.

5. Agriculture

(On the South, see also 83.5–84.20.)

6 ABBOT, Richard H. "The Agricultural Press Views the Yeoman, 1819–1859." *Ag Hist,* XLII(1968):35–48. (Examines the "agrarian myth.")

7 BARDOLPH, Richard. *Agricultural Literature and the Early Illinois Farmer.* Stud Soc Sci (Ill), XXIX. Urbana, Ill., 1948.

8 BIDWELL, Percy Wells, and John I. FALCONER. *History of Agriculture in the Northern United States, 1620–1860. Car Inst Pub,* No. 358. Washington, 1925.

9 BOGUE, Allan G. *From Prairie to Corn Belt: Farming on the Illinois and Iowa Prairies in the Nineteenth Century.* Chicago, 1963.†

10 BONNER, James C. "Genesis of Agricultural Reform in the Cotton Belt." *J S Hist,* IX(1943):475–500.

11 BONNER, James C. *A History of Georgia Agriculture, 1732–1860.* Athens, Ga., 1964.

12 BRUCHEY, Stuart, ed. *Cotton and the Growth of the American Economy, 1790–1860: Sources and Readings.* New York, 1967.†

13 CATHEY, Cornelius Oliver. *Agricultural Developments in North Carolina, 1783–1860.* Chapel Hill, N.C., 1956.

14 CLARK, Blanche H. *The Tennessee Yeoman, 1840–1860.* Nashville, 1942.

15 CLARK, John G. *The Grain Trade in the Old Northwest.* Urbana, Ill., 1966.

16 COLE, Arthur Harrison. *Wholesale Commodity Prices in the United States, 1700–1861.* Cambridge, Mass., 1938.

17 CRAVEN, Avery. *Soil Exhaustion as a Factor in the Agricultural History of Virginia and Maryland. Stud Soc Sci* (Ill), XIII. Urbana, Ill., 1925.

18 DAVIS, Charles S. *The Cotton Kingdom in Alabama.* Montgomery, Ala., 1939.

1   DEMAREE, Albert L. *The American Agricultural Press, 1819–1860.* New York, 1941.

2   GATES, Paul Wallace. *The Farmer's Age.* See 38.5.

3   GRAY, Lewis Cecil. *History of Agriculture in the Southern United States to 1860. Car Inst Pub,* No. 430. 2 vols. Washington, 1933.

4   HEDRICK, U. P. *A History of Horticulture in America to 1860.* New York, 1950.

5   HENLEIN, Paul C. *Cattle Kingdom in the Ohio Valley, 1783–1860.* Lexington, Ky., 1959.

6   HOPKINS, James F. *A History of the Hemp Industry in Kentucky.* Lexington, Ky., 1951.

7   HOUSE, Albert Virgil, ed. *Planter Management and Capitalism in Ante-Bellum Georgia: The Journal of Hugh Fraser Grant, Ricegrower.* New York, 1954. (80-page introduction is especially useful.)

8   JORDAN, Weymouth T. *Hugh Davis and His Alabama Plantation.* University, Ala., 1948.

9   KEMMERER, Donald L. "The Pre-Civil War South's Leading Crop, Corn." *Ag Hist,* XXIII(1949):236–239.

10   MOORE, John H. *Agriculture in Ante-Bellum Mississippi.* New York, 1958.

11   NEELY, Wayne Caldwell. *The Agricultural Fair.* New York, 1935.

12   PABST, Margaret Richards. *Agricultural Trends in the Connecticut Valley Region of Massachusetts, 1800–1900. Stud Hist* (Smith), XXVI. Northampton, Mass., 1941.

13   ROBERT, Joseph C. *The Tobacco Kingdom: Plantation, Market, and Factory in Virginia and North Carolina, 1800–1860.* Durham, N.C., 1938.

14   ROTHSTEIN, Morton. "Antebellum Wheat and Cotton Exports: Contrast in Marketing Organization and Economic Development." *Ag Hist,* XL(1966), 91–100.

15   SCHMIDT, Louis Bernard. "The Internal Grain Trade of the United States, 1850–1860." *Iowa J Hist Pol,* XVIII(1920):94–124.

16   SITTERSON, J. Carlyle. *Sugar Country: The Cane Sugar Industry in the South, 1753–1950.* Lexington, Ky., 1953.

17   SMITH, Alfred Glaze, Jr. *Economic Readjustment of an Old Cotton State: South Carolina, 1820–1860.* Columbia, S.C., 1958.†

18   TAYLOR, Henry C., and Anne Dewees TAYLOR. *The Story of Agricultural Economics in the United States, 1840–1932.* Ames, Iowa, 1952.

19   WEAVER, Herbert. *Mississippi Farmers, 1850–1860.* Nashville, 1945.

6. *Industry and Commerce*

A. *General*

1 BISHOP, J. Leander. *A History of American Manufactures from 1608 to 1860.* 3 vols. Philadelphia, 1861–1868. (Old, but a mine of information.)

2 CLARK, Victor S. *History of Manufactures in the United States.* 3 vols. New York, 1929. (Particularly, Vol. I.)

3 EVANS, G. Heberton, Jr. *Business Incorporations in the United States, 1800–1943.* New York, 1948.

4 JOHNSON, Emory R., et al. *History of Domestic and Foreign Commerce of the United States. Car Inst Pub,* No. 215A. Washington, 1915.

5 SCHMIDT, Louis Bernard. "Internal Commerce and the Development of National Economy before 1860." *J Pol Econ,* XLVII(1939):798–822.

6 TRYON, Rolla Milton. *Household Manufactures in the United States, 1640–1860.* Chicago, 1917.

B. *Special Topics*

7 CARSON, Gerald. *The Old Country Store.* New York, 1954.

8 COCHRAN, Thomas C. *Railroad Leaders, 1845–1890: The Business Mind in Action.* Cambridge, Mass., 1953. (Partly letters.)

9 COLE, Arthur Harrison. *The American Wool Manufacture.* 2 vols. Cambridge, Mass., 1926.

10 DAVIS, Pearce. *The Development of the American Glass Industry.* Cambridge, Mass., 1949.

11 JONES, Fred Mitchell. *Middlemen in the Domestic Trade of the United States, 1800–1860. Stud Soc Sci* (Ill), XXI. Urbana, Ill., 1937.

12 LYNN, Robert A. "Installment Credit before 1870." *Bus Hist Rev,* XXXI(1957):414–424.

13 MOMENT, David. "The Business of Whaling in America in the 1850's." *Bus Hist Rev,* XXXI(1957):261–291.

14 TEMIN, Peter. *Iron and Steel in Nineteenth Century America: An Economic Inquiry.* Cambridge, Mass., 1964.

15 WOODMAN, Harold D. *King Cotton and His Retainers: Financing and Marketing the Cotton Crop of the South, 1800–1925.* Lexington, Ky., 1968.

C. *Regional, State, and Local Studies*
(Listed geographically by regions and states)

16 DAVIS, Lance Edwin. "Stock Ownership in the Early New England Textile Industry." *Bus Hist Rev,* XXXII(1958):204–222.

1 MC GOULDRICK, Paul F. *New England Textiles in the Nineteenth Century: Profits and Investment.* Cambridge, Mass., 1968.

2 WARE, Caroline F. *The Early New England Cotton Manufacture.* Boston, 1931.

3 COPELAND, Jennie F. *Every Day but Sunday: The Romantic Age of New England Industry.* Brattleboro, Vt., 1936. (On Mansfield, Mass.)

4 DEYRUP, Felicia Johnson. *Arms Makers of the Connecticut Valley . . . 1798– 1870. Stud Hist* (Smith), XXXIII. Northampton, Mass., 1948.

5 DODD, Edwin Merrick. *American Business Corporations until 1860, with Special Reference to Massachusetts.* Cambridge, Mass., 1954.

6 HAZARD, Blanche Evans. *The Organization of the Boot and Shoe Industry in Massachusetts before 1875.* Cambridge, Mass., 1921.

7 MORISON, Samuel Eliot. *The Maritime History of Massachusetts, 1783– 1860.* Boston, 1921.†

8 SCHLAKMAN, Vera. *Economic History of a Factory Town: A Study of Chicopee, Massachusetts. Stud Hist* (Smith), XX. Northampton, Mass., 1935.

9 ALBION, Robert G. *The Rise of New York Port, 1815–1860.* New York, 1939.

10 EISELEN, Malcolm Rogers. *The Rise of Pennsylvania Protectionism.* Philadelphia, 1932.

11 HUNTER, Louis C. "Financial Problems of the Early Pittsburgh Iron Manufacturers." *J Econ Bus Hist*, II(1930):520–544.

12 HUNTER, Louis C. "Influence of the Market upon Technique in the Iron Industry in Western Pennsylvania up to 1860." *J Econ Bus Hist*, I(1929):241– 281.

13 ATHERTON, Lewis. *The Southern Country Store, 1800–1860.* Baton Rouge, La., 1949.

14 VAN DEUSEN, John G. *Ante-Bellum Southern Commercial Conventions.* Durham, N.C., 1926.

15 WENDER, Herbert. *Southern Commercial Conventions, 1837–1859. Stud Hist Pol Sci* (Hop), XLVIII. Baltimore, 1930.

16 LANDER, Ernest M., Jr. *The Textile Industry in Antebellum South Carolina* Baton Rouge, 1969.

17 CLARK, John G. "New Orleans and the River: A Study in Attitudes and Responses." *La Hist*, VIII(1967):117–135.

18 SUAREZ, Raleigh A. "Bargains, Bills and Bankruptcies: Business Activity in Rural Antebellum Louisiana." *La Hist*, VII(1966):189–206.

19 HUNTER, Louis C. *Studies in the Economic History of the Ohio Valley. Stud Hist* (Smith), XIX. Northampton, Mass., 1934.

20 KOHLMEIER, Albert L. *The Old Northwest as the Keystone of the Arch of American Federal Union: A Study in Commerce and Politics.* Bloomington, Ind., 1938.

1 BERRY, Thomas Senior. *Western Prices before 1861: A Study of the Cincinnati Market.* Cambridge, Mass., 1943.

2 BELCHER, Wyatt Winton. *The Economic Rivalry between St. Louis and Chicago, 1850–1880.* New York, 1947.

3 FRIES, Robert F. *Empire in Pine: The Story of Lumbering in Wisconsin, 1830–1900.* Madison, Wis., 1951.

4 CAROSSO, Vincent P. *The California Wine Industry, 1830–1895.* Berkeley, 1951.

5 THROCKMORTON, Arthur L. *Oregon Argonauts.* See 14.11.

D. *Individual Companies and Men*

6 EWING, John S., and Nancy P. NORTON. *Broadlooms and Businessmen: A History of the Bigelow-Sanford Carpet Company.* Cambridge, Mass., 1955.

7 GIBB, George Sweet. *The Whitesmiths of Taunton: A History of Reed and Barton, 1824–1943.* Cambridge, Mass., 1946.

8 HUTCHINSON, William T. *Cyrus Hall McCormick.* 2 vols. New York, 1930–1935.

9 KNOWLTON, Evelyn H. *Pepperell's Progress: History of a Cotton Textile Company, 1844–1945.* Cambridge, Mass., 1948.

10 MITCHELL, Broadus. *William Gregg, Factory Master of the Old South.* Chapel Hill, N.C., 1928.

11 NEU, Irene D. *Erastus Corning, Merchant and Financier, 1794–1872.* Ithaca, N.Y., 1960.

12 NEVINS, Allan. *Abram S. Hewitt, with Some Account of Peter Cooper.* New York, 1935.

13 NORRIS, James D. *Frontier Iron: The Maramec Iron Works, 1826–1876.* Madison, Wis., 1964. (In Missouri.)

14 WYATT-BROWN, Bertram. "God and Dun & Bradstreet, 1841–1851." *Bus Hist Rev,* XL(1966):432–450.

7. Transportation and Communication
(See also 16.19–17.20.)

A. *General*

15 DUNBAR, Seymour. *A History of Travel in America.* 4 vols. Indianapolis, 1915. (Particularly, Vols. III and IV.)

16 GOODRICH, Carter. *Government Promotion of American Canals and Railroads, 1800–1890.* New York, 1960.

17 GOODRICH, Carter. "Revulsion against Internal Improvements." *J Econ Hist,* X(1950), 145–169.

18 HILL, Forest G. *Roads, Rails, and Waterways: The Army Engineers and Early Transportation.* Norman, Okla., 1957.

19 KIRKLAND, Edward Chase. *Men, Cities, and Transportation: A Study in New England History, 1820–1900.* 2 vols. Cambridge, Mass., 1948.

1 KRENKEL, John H. *Illinois Internal Improvements, 1818–1848.* Cedar Rapids, Iowa, 1958.

2 LANE, Wheaton J. *From Indian Trail to Iron Horse: Travel and Transportation in New Jersey, 1620–1860.* Princeton, 1939.

3 MEYER, Balthasar Henry, ed., with Caroline E. MAC GILL et al. *History of Transportation in the United States before 1860. Car Inst Pub*, No. 215C. Washington, 1917.

4 PHILLIPS, Ulrich Bonnell. *A History of Transportation in the Eastern Cotton Belt to 1860.* New York, 1908.

B. Ocean Transportation

5 ALBION, Robert G. *Square Riggers on Schedule: The New York Sailing Packets to England, France, and the Cotton Ports.* Princeton, 1938.

6 BOWEN, Frank C. *A Century of Atlantic Travel, 1830–1930.* Boston, 1930.

7 CUTLER, Carl C. *Greyhounds of the Sea: The Story of the American Clipper Ship.* New York, 1930.

8 CUTLER, Carl C. *Queens of the Western Ocean: The Story of America's Mail and Passenger Sailing Lines.* Annapolis, 1961.

9 HUTCHINS, John G. B. *The American Maritime Industries and Public Policy, 1789–1914.* Cambridge, Mass., 1941.

10 LANE, Wheaton J. *Commodore Vanderbilt: An Epic of the Steam Age.* New York, 1942.

11 MORISON, Samuel Eliot. *The Maritime History of Massachusetts.* See 44.7.

12 TYLER, David B. *Steam Conquers the Atlantic.* New York, 1939.

C. Inland Waterways and Roads

13 AMBLER, Charles H. *History of Transportation in the Ohio Valley.* Glendale, Calif., 1932.

14 CLEMENS, Samuel L. [Mark Twain]. *Life on the Mississippi.* Boston, 1883.†

15 COLE, Harry Ellsworth. *Stagecoach and Tavern Tales of the Old Northwest,* Ed. by Louise Phelps Kellogg. Cleveland, 1930.

16 GOODRICH, Carter, ed. *Canals and American Economic Development.* New York, 1961. (Essays by four scholars.)

17 GRAY, Ralph D. *The National Waterway: A History of the Chesapeake and Delaware Canal, 1769–1965.* Urbana, Ill., 1967.

18 HARTSOUGH, Mildred L. *From Canoe to Steel Barge on the Upper Mississippi.* Minneapolis, 1934.

19 HUNTER, Louis C. *Steamboats on the Western Waters: An Economic and Technological History.* Cambridge, Mass., 1949.

1 JORDAN, Philip D. *The National Road.* Indianapolis, 1948.

2 PETERSEN, William J. *Steamboating on the Upper Mississippi: The Water Way to Iowa.* Iowa City, 1937.

3 PUTNAM, James W. *The Illinois and Michigan Canal: A Study in Economic History.* Chicago, 1918.

4 QUAIFE, Milo Milton. *Chicago's Highways, Old and New.* Chicago, 1923.

5 RANSOM, Roger L. "Interregional Canals and Economic Specialization in the Antebellum United States." *Explor Entrepren Hist* [2nd Ser], V(1967), 12–35.

6 SANDERLIN, Walter S. *The Great National Project: A History of the Chesapeake and Ohio Canal.* Baltimore, 1946.

7 SCHEIBER, Harry. *Ohio Canal Era: A Case Study of Government and the Economy, 1820–1861.* Athens, Ohio, 1968.

8 SHAW, Ronald E. *Erie Water West: A History of the Erie Canal, 1792–1854.* Lexington, Ky., 1966.

9 WAGGONER, Madeline Sadler. *The Long Haul West: The Great Canal Era, 1817–1850.* New York, 1958.

10 WILLIAMS, Mentor L. "The Chicago River and Harbor Convention, 1847." *Miss Val Hist Rev*, XXXV(1949):607–626.

D. Railroads

11 BOGLE, Victor M. "Railroad Building in Indiana, 1850–55." *Ind Mag Hist*, LVIII(1962):211–232.

12 BROWN, Cecil Kenneth. *A State Movement in Railroad Development.* Chapel Hill, N.C., 1928. (North Carolina.)

13 CHANDLER, Alfred D., Jr. "Patterns of American Railroad Finance, 1830–50." *Bus Hist Rev*, XXVIII(1954):248–263.

14 CLARK, Thomas D. *The Beginning of the L & N: The Development of the Louisville and Nashville Railroad and Its Memphis Branches from 1836 to 1860.* Louisville, 1933.

15 CLARK, Thomas D. *A Pioneer Southern Railroad from New Orleans to Cairo.* Chapel Hill, N.C., 1936.

16 CORLISS, Carlton J. *Main Line of Mid-America: The Story of the Illinois Central.* New York, 1950.

17 COTTERILL, Robert S. "Southern Railroads and Western Trade, 1840–1850." *Miss Val Hist Rev*, III(1917):427–441.

18 COTTERILL, Robert S. "Southern Railroads, 1850–1860." *Miss Val Hist Rev*, X(1924):396–405.

19 FISH, Carl Russell. "The Northern Railroads, April, 1861." *Am Hist Rev*, XXII(1917):778–793.

20 FISHLOW, Albert. *American Railroads and the Transformation of the Ante-Bellum Economy.* Cambridge, Mass., 1965.

21 FOGEL, Robert William. *Railroads and American Economic Growth: Essays in Econometric History.* Baltimore, 1964.

1   GATES, Paul Wallace. *The Illinois Central Railroad*. See 16.8.

2   HANEY, Lewis Henry. *A Congressional History of Railroads in the United States to 1850*. *Econ Pol Sci Ser* (Wis), III. Madison, Wis., 1908.

3   HUNGERFORD, Edward. *Men of Erie*. New York, 1946.

4   HUNGERFORD, Edward. *The Story of the Baltimore & Ohio Railroad, 1827–1927*. 2 vols. New York, 1928.

5   JOHNSON, Arthur M., and Barry E. SUPPLE. *Boston Capitalists and Western Railroads: A Study in the Nineteenth-Century Railroad Investment Process*. Cambridge, Mass., 1967.

6   KENNEDY, Charles J. "Commuter Services in the Boston Area, 1835–1860." *Bus Hist Rev*, XXXVI(1962):153–170.

7   MORGAN, Edward James. "Sources of Capital for Railroads in the Old Northwest before the Civil War." Doctoral dissertation, University of Wisconsin, 1964.

8   OVERTON, Richard C. *Burlington Route: A History of the Burlington Lines*. New York, 1965.

9   REED, Merl E. *New Orleans and the Railroads: The Struggle for Commercial Empire, 1830–1860*. Baton Rouge, 1966.

10 RIEGEL, Robert Edgar. *The Story of the Western Railroads, from 1852 through the Reign of the Giants*. New York, 1926.†

11 RIEGEL, Robert Edgar. "Trans-Mississippi Railroads during the Fifties." *Miss Val Hist Rev*, X(1923):152–172.

12 SALSBURY, Stephen. *The State, the Investor, and the Railroad: The Boston & Albany, 1825–1867*. Cambridge, Mass., 1967.

13 STEVENS, Frank Walker. *The Beginnings of the New York Central Railroad*. New York, 1926.

14 STOVER, John F. *American Railroads*. Chicago, 1961.†

15 TAYLOR, George Rogers, and Irene D. NEU. *The American Railroad Network, 1861–1890*. Cambridge, Mass., 1956. (Gives a detailed description of the railroad system in 1861.)

E.   Communication

16 HARLOW, Alvin F. *Old Post Bags*. See 29.5.

17 HARLOW, Alvin F. *Old Waybills: The Romance of the Express Companies*. New York, 1934.

18 HARLOW, Alvin F. *Old Wires and New Waves: The History of the Telegraph, Telephone, and Wireless*. New York, 1936.

19 MABEE, Carleton. *The American Leonardo*. See 40.14.

20 THOMPSON, Robert L. *Wiring a Continent: The History of the Telegraph Industry in the United States, 1832–1866*. Princeton, 1947.

8. *Financial Institutions and Business Cycles*

21 BRAYER, Herbert O. "Insurance against the Hazards of Western Life." *Miss Val Hist Rev*, XXXIV(1947):221–236.

1 CALDWELL, Stephen A. *A Banking History of Louisiana*. Baton Rouge, 1935.

2 CHADDOCK, Robert E. *The Safety Fund Banking System in New York State, 1829–1866*. Pub Nat Mon Comm, IV. Washington, 1910.

3 CLOUGH, Shepard B. *A Century of American Life Insurance: A History of the Mutual Life Insurance Company of New York, 1843–1943*. New York, 1946.

4 DEWEY, Davis Rich. *Financial History of the United States*. New York, 1903. (Many subsequent editions.)

5 ERICKSON, Erling Arthur. "Banks and Politics before the Civil War: The Case of Iowa, 1836–1865." Doctoral dissertation, University of Iowa, 1967.

6 EZELL, John Samuel. *Fortune's Merry Wheel: The Lottery in America*. Cambridge, Mass., 1960.

7 GIBBONS, J. S. *The Banks of New-York, Their Dealers, the Clearing House, and the Panic of 1857*. New York, 1859.

8 HAMMOND, Bray. *Banks and Politics in America, from the Revolution to the Civil War*. Princeton, 1957.†

9 HENDRICK, Burton J. *The Story of Life Insurance*. New York, 1907.

10 HEDGES, Joseph Edward. *Commercial Banking and the Stock Market before 1863*. Stud Hist Pol Sci (Hop), LVI. Baltimore, 1938.

11 HIDY, Ralph W. *The House of Baring in American Trade and Finance: English Merchant Bankers at Work, 1763–1861*. Cambridge, Mass., 1949.

12 HUGHES, J. R. T., and Nathan ROSENBERG. "The United States Business Cycle before 1860: Some Problems of Interpretation." *Econ Hist Rev*, XV(1963):476–493.

13 JAMES, F. Cyril. *The Growth of Chicago Banks*. 2 vols. New York, 1938.

14 KINLEY, David. *The Independent Treasury of the United States and Its Relation to the Banks of the Country*. Pub Nat Mon Comm, VII. Washington, 1910.

15 MILLER, Harry E. *Banking Theories in the United States before 1860*. Cambridge, Mass., 1927.

16 MYERS, Margaret G. *Origins and Developments*. Vol. I of *The New York Money Market*. 4 vols. New York, 1931–1932.

17 REDLICH, Fritz. *The Molding of American Banking: Men and Ideas*. Vol. II of *History of American Business Leaders*. 2 vols. New York, 1951.

18 REZNECK, Samuel. "The Influence of Depression upon American Opinion 1857–1859." *J Econ Hist*, II(1942):1–23.

19 SHARP, James Roger. "Banking and Politics in the States: The Democratic Party after the Panic of 1837." Doctoral dissertation, University of California, 1966. (Emphasis on Virginia, Ohio, and Mississippi.)

20 SMITH, Alice Elizabeth. *George Smith's Money: A Scottish Investor in America*. Madison, Wis., 1966.

1 SMITH, Arthur A. "Bank Note Detecting in the Era of State Banks." *Miss Val Hist Rev*, XXIX(1942):371–386.

2 SMITH, Walter Buckingham, and Arthur Harrison COLE. *Fluctuations in American Business, 1790–1860*. Cambridge, Mass., 1935.

3 STUDENSKI, Paul, and Herman E. KROOSS. *Financial History of the United States*. 2nd ed. New York, 1963.

4 TAUS, Esther Rogoff. *Central Banking Functions of the United States Treasury, 1789–1941*. New York, 1943.

5 VAN VLECK, George Washington. *The Panic of 1857: An Analytical Study*. New York, 1943.

6 WHITE, Gerald T. *A History of the Massachusetts Hospital Life Insurance Company*. Cambridge, Mass., 1955.

9. Government and the Economy

7 BEARD, Earl S. "Local Aid to Railroads in Iowa." *Iowa J Hist*, L(1952):1–34.

8 GOODRICH, Carter. *Government Promotion* .... See 45.16.

9 GOODRICH, Carter. "The Virginia System of Mixed Enterprise: A Study of State Planning of Internal Improvements." *Pol Sci Q*, LXIV (1949), 355–387.

10 HANDLIN, Oscar, and Mary Flug HANDLIN. *Commonwealth, a Study of the Role of Government in the American Economy: Massachusetts, 1774–1861*. New York, 1947.

11 HARTZ, Louis. *Economic Policy and Democratic Thought: Pennsylvania, 1776–1860*. Cambridge, Mass., 1948.†

12 HEATH, Milton S. *Constructive Liberalism: The Role of the State in Economic Development in Georgia to 1860*. Cambridge, Mass., 1954.

13 HILL, Forest G. "Government Engineering Aid to Railroads before the Civil War." *J Econ Hist*, XI(1951):235–246.

14 HILL, Forest G. *Roads, Rails, and Waterways*. See 45.18.

15 HUTCHINS, John G. B. *The American Maritime Industries* .... See 46.9.

16 KLEBANER, Benjamin J. "Poor Relief and Public Works During the Depression of 1857." *Historian*, XXII(1960):264–279.

17 LIVELY, Robert A. "The American System: A Review Article." *Bus Hist Rev*, XXIX(1955):81–96.

18 NASH, Gerald D. *State Government and Economic Development: A History of Administration Policies in California, 1849–1933*. Berkeley, 1964.

19 PRIMM, James N. *Economic Policy in the Development of a Western State: Missouri, 1820–1860*. Cambridge, Mass., 1954.

20 SALSBURY, Stephen. *The State, the Investor, and the Railroad*. See 48.12.

1   SCHEIBER, Harry. *Ohio Canal Era.* See 47.7.

2   STANWOOD, Edward. *American Tariff Controversies in the Nineteenth Century.* 2 vols. Boston, 1903.

3   TAUSSIG, F. W. *The Tariff History of the United States.* 6th ed. New York 1914.

4   WARREN, Charles. *Bankruptcy in United States History.* Cambridge, Mass., 1935.

5   WRIGHT, James E. *The Galena Lead District: Federal Policy and Practice, 1824–1847.* Madison, Wis., 1966.

10. Labor

6   COMMONS, John R. et al. *History of Labour in the United States.* 4 vols. New York, 1918–1935. (Particularly, Vol. I.)

7   DEGLER, Carl N. "Labor in the Economy and Politics of New York City, 1850–1860." Doctoral dissertation, Columbia University, 1952.

8   ERNST, Robert. "Economic Nativism in New York City during the 1840's." *N Y Hist,* XXIX(1948):170–186.

9   GINGER, Ray. "Labor in a Massachusetts Cotton Mill, 1853–1860." *Bus Hist Rev,* XXVIII(1954):67–91.

10 GROSSMAN, Jonathan. *William Sylvis, Pioneer of American Labor.* New York, 1948.

11 LOFTON, Williston H. "Abolition and Labor." *J Neg Hist,* XXXIII(1948): 249–283.

12 PERSONS, Charles E. "The Early History of Factory Legislation in Massachusetts." *Labor Laws and Their Enforcement.* Ed. by Susan M. Kingsbury. *Stud Econ Rel Women,* II. New York, 1911.

13 RAYBACK, Joseph G. "The American Workingman and the Antislavery Crusade." *J Econ Hist,* III(1943):152–163.

14 WARE, Norman J. *The Industrial Worker, 1840–1860.* Boston, 1924.†

15 ZAHLER, Helene Sara. *Eastern Workingmen . . . .* See 16.18.

V. American Society

1. Bibliography and Historiography

16 BOWERS, David F., ed. *Foreign Influences in American Life.* Princeton, 1944. (Bibliography: pp. 175–254.)

17 BURR, Nelson R. *A Critical Bibliography of Religion in America.* 2 vols., designated Vol. IV, Parts 1–2 and 3–5, of *Religion in American Life,* ed. by James Ward Smith and A. Leland Jamison. Princeton, 1961. (Exhaustive.)

1 CREMIN, Lawrence A. *The Wonderful World of Ellwood Patterson Cubberley: An Essay on the Historiography of American Education.* New York, 1965.

2 EGBERT, Donald Drew, and Stow PERSONS. *Socialism and Amercan Life.* 2 vols. Princeton, 1952. (Particularly, Vol. II: *Bibliography,* T. D. Seymour Bassett, bibliographer.)

3 ELLIS, John Tracy. *A Guide to American Catholic History.* Milwaukee, 1959.

4 HARLAN, Louis R. *The Negro in American History.* Washington, 1965. (Service Center for Teachers of History pamphlet.)

5 SALK, Erwin A. *A Layman's Guide to Negro History.* 2nd ed. New York, 1967.

6 WELSCH, Erwin K. *The Negro in the United States: A Research Guide.* Bloomington, Ind., 1965.†

2. Selected Source Materials

7 APTHEKER, Herbert, ed. *A Documentary History of the Negro People in the United States.* New York, 1951.†

8 BILLINGTON, Ray Allen, ed. *The Journal of Charlotte L. Forten, a Free Negro in the Slave Era.* New York, 1953. (1854 to 1864.)

9 BLEGEN, Theodore C., ed. *Land of Their Choice: The Immigrants Write Home.* Minneapolis, 1955. (Norwegian.)

10 BODE, Carl, ed. *American Life in the 1840's.* Garden City, N.Y., 1967.†

11 *A Century of Population Growth: From the First Census of the United States to the Twelfth, 1790–1900.* Washington, 1909.

12 COMMAGER, Henry Steele, ed. *The Era of Reform, 1830–1860.* Princeton, 1960.†

13 FONER, Philip S. *The Life and Writings of Frederick Douglass.* 4 vols. New York, 1950–1955.†

14 FREEDMAN, Florence Bernstein, ed. *Walt Whitman Looks at the Schools.* New York, 1950. (Whitman's journalistic comment, 1845–1848.)

15 HOFSTADTER, Richard, and Wilson SMITH, eds. *American Higher Education: A Documentary History.* 2 vols. Chicago, 1961.

16 HOGAN, William Ransom, and Edwin Adams DAVIS, eds. *William Johnson's Natchez: The Ante-Bellum Diary of a Free Negro.* Baton Rouge, 1951.

17 KNIGHT, Edgar W., ed. *A Documentary History of Education in the South before 1860.* 5 vols. Chapel Hill, N.C., 1949–1953.

18 RATNER, Lorman, ed. *Pre-Civil War Reform: The Variety of Principles and Programs.* Englewood Cliffs, N.J., 1967.†

19 SMITH, H. Shelton, Robert T. HANDY, and Lefferts A. LOETSCHER. *American Christianity: An Historical Interpretation with Representative Documents.* 2 vols. New York, 1960–1963.

1 STOKES, Anson Phelps. *Church and State in the United States.* 3 vols. New York, 1950. (Historical survey and source book; particularly, Vol. II.)

2 WOODSON, Carter G., ed. *The Mind of the Negro as Reflected in Letters Written during the Crisis, 1800–1860.* Washington, 1926.

3. General Studies

3 BERTHOFF, Rowland. "The American Social Order: A Conservative Hypothesis." *Am Hist Rev,* LXV(1960):495–514.

4 BRANCH, Edward Douglas. *The Sentimental Years, 1836–1860.* New York, 1934.†

5 BRIGHTFIELD, Myron F. "America and the Americans, 1840–1860, as Depicted in English Novels of the Period." *Am Lit,* XXXI(1959):309–324.

6 COLE, Arthur Charles. *The Irrepressible Conflict, 1850–1865.* New York, 1934. (Vol. VII in the notable 13-volume social history, "A History of American Life," ed. by Arthur M. Schlesinger and Dixon Ryan Fox.)

7 DICK, Everett. *The Dixie Frontier: A Social History of the Southern Frontier from the First Transmontane Beginnings to the Civil War.* New York, 1948.†

8 FARNAM, Henry W. *Chapters in the History of Social Legislation in the United States to 1860.* Ed. by Clive Day. *Car Inst Pub,* No. 488. Washington, 1938.

9 FISH, Carl Russell. *The Rise of the Common Man, 1830–1850.* New York, 1927. (Vol. VI in "A History of American Life.")

10 GLAAB, Charles N., and A. Theodore BROWN. *A History of Urban America.* New York, 1967.

11 HIGHAM, John. *From Boundlessness to Consolidation: The Transformation of American Culture, 1848–1860.* Ann Arbor, Mich., 1969. (Pamphlet.)

12 MILLER, Douglas T. *Jacksonian Aristocracy.* See 39.1.

13 NICHOLS, Thomas Law. *Forty Years of American Life, 1821–1861.* New York, 1937. (Originally published in 1864.)

14 PATTEE, Fred Lewis. *The Feminine Fifties.* New York, 1940.

15 TYLER, Alice Felt. *Freedom's Ferment: Phases of American Social History to 1860.* Minneapolis, 1944.†

16 WISH, Harvey. *Society and Thought in Early America.* New York, 1950.

17 WRIGHT, Louis B. *Culture on the Moving Frontier.* Bloomington, Ind., 1955.†

4. Population, Immigration, and Nativism

A. General

18 BEALS, Carleton. *Brass-Knuckle Crusade: The Great Know-Nothing Conspiracy, 1820–1860.* New York, 1960. (Colorful but extreme.)

1 BILLINGTON, Ray Allen. *The Protestant Crusade, 1800–1860*. New York 1938.†

2 CARMAN, Harry J., and Reinhard H. LUTHIN. "Some Aspects of the Know-Nothing Movement Reconsidered." *S Atl Q*, XXXIX (1940): 213–234.

3 DAVIS, David Brion. "Some Ideological Functions of Prejudice in Antebellum America." *Am Q*, XV (1963): 115–125.

4 DAVIS, David Brion. "Some Themes of Counter-Subversion: An Analysis of Anti-Masonic, Anti-Catholic, and Anti-Mormon Literature." *Miss Val Hist Rev*, XLVII(1960):205–224.

5 GREENWALD, William I. "The Ante-Bellum Population, 1830–1860." *Mid-Am*, XXXVI(1954):176–189.

6 HANDLIN, Oscar. *The Uprooted*. Boston, 1951.† (Classic study of the immigrant's problems of adjustment.)

7 HANSEN, Marcus Lee. *The Atlantic Migration, 1607–1860*. Ed. by Arthur M. Schlesinger. Cambridge, Mass., 1940.†

8 HARPER, Richard Conant. "The Course of the Melting Pot Idea to 1910." Doctoral dissertation, Columbia University, 1968.

9 HOLBROOK, Stewart H. *The Yankee Exodus: An Account of Migration from New England*. New York, 1950.†

10 JONES, Maldwyn Allen. *American Immigration*. Chicago, 1960.†

11 NIEBUHR, H. Richard. *The Social Sources of Denominationalism*. New York, 1929. (Particularly, Chapter VIII: "The Churches of the Immigrants.")

12 OVERDYKE, W. Darrell. *The Know-Nothing Party in the South*. See 31.17.

13 POWER, Richard Lyle. *Planting Corn Belt Culture: The Impress of the Upland Southerner and Yankee in the Old Northwest*. Indianapolis, 1953.

14 SPENGLER, Joseph J. "Population Theory in the Ante-Bellum South." *J S Hist*, II(1936):360–389.

15 STEPHENSON, George M. *A History of American Immigration, 1820–1924*. Boston, 1926.

16 STEPHENSON, George M. "Nativism in the Forties and Fifties, with Special Reference to the Mississippi Valley." *Miss Val Hist Rev*, IX(1922):185–202.

17 THOMAS, Brinley. *Migration and Economic Growth: A Study of Great Britain and the Atlantic Economy*. Cambridge, England, 1954.

18 THOMAS, M. Evangeline. *Nativism in the Old Northwest, 1850–1860*. Washington, 1936.

19 THOMPSON, Warren S., and P. K. WHELPTON. *Population Trends in the United States*. New York, 1933.

20 WITTKE, Carl. *We Who Built America: The Saga of the Immigrant*. New York, 1939.†

B. Special Groups

1 BARTH, Gunther. *Bitter Strength: A History of the Chinese in the United States, 1850–1870*. Cambridge, Mass., 1964.

2 BERTHOFF, Rowland. *British Immigrants in Industrial America, 1790–1950*. Cambridge, Mass., 1953.

3 BLEGEN, Theodore C. *Norwegian Migration to America, 1825–1860*. Northfield, Minn., 1931.

4 HANSEN, Marcus Lee. *The Mingling of the Canadian and American Peoples* New Haven, Conn., 1940. (Completed by John Bartlett Brebner.)

5 HAWGOOD, John A. *The Tragedy of German-America*. New York, 1940.

6 JANSON, Florence E. *The Background of Swedish Immigration, 1840–1930* Chicago, 1931.

7 KELLY, Mary Gilbert. *Catholic Immigrant Colonization Projects in the United States, 1815–1860* New York, 1939.

8 LEVINE, Edward M. *The Irish and Irish Politicians*. Notre Dame, Ind., 1966.

9 LUCAS, Henry S. *Netherlanders in America: Dutch Immigration to the United States and Canada, 1789–1950*. Ann Arbor, Mich., 1955.

10 MULDER, William. *Homeward to Zion*. See 22.9.

11 OLSSON, Nils William, ed. *A Pioneer in Northwest America, 1841–1858: The Memoirs of Gustaf Unonius*. Trans. by Jonas Oscar Backlund. 2 vols. Minneapolis, 1950.

12 POTTER, George W. *To the Golden Door: The Story of the Irish in Ireland and America*. Boston, 1960.

13 QUALEY, Carlton C. *Norwegian Settlement in the United States*. Northfield Minn., 1938.

14 SHEPPERSON, W. E. *British Emigration to North America: Projects and Opinions in the Early Victorian Period*. Minneapolis, 1957.

15 WITTKE, Carl F. *The Irish in America*. Baton Rouge, 1956.

16 WITTKE, Carl F. *Refugees of Revolution: The German Forty-Eighters in America*. Philadelphia, 1952.

17 WOODHAM-SMITH, Cecil. *The Great Hunger: Ireland, 1845–9*. London, 1962. (The potato famine.)

18 ZUCKER, Adolf E., ed. *The Forty-Eighters, Political Refugees of the German Revolution of 1848*. New York, 1950. (Anthology of essays.)

C. State and Local Studies
(For political nativism, see 32.15–35.20.)

19 CHENAULT, William W., and Robert C. REINDERS. "The Northern-Born Community of New Orleans in the 1850's." *J Am Hist*, LI(1964):232–247.

20 ERNST, Robert. "Economic Nativism in New York City . . . ." See 51.8.

1 ERNST, Robert. *Immigrant Life in New York City, 1825–1863.* New York, 1949.

2 GIBSON, Florence E. *The Attitudes of the New York Irish toward State and National Affairs, 1848–1892.* New York, 1951.

3 HANDLIN, Oscar. *Boston's Immigrants, 1790–1865: A Study in Acculturation.* Cambridge, Mass., 1941.†

4 NIEHAUS, Earl F. *The Irish in New Orleans, 1800–1860.* Baton Rouge, 1965.

5 PITT, Leonard. "The Beginnings of Nativism in California." *Pac Hist Rev,* XXX(1961):23–38.

6 PITT, Leonard. *The Decline of the Californios: A Social History of the Spanish-Speaking Californians, 1846–1890.* Berkeley, 1966.

7 STILWELL, Lewis D. *Migration from Vermont, 1776–1860.* Montpelier, Vt., 1937.

8 THRONE, Mildred. "A Population Study of an Iowa County in 1850." *Iowa J Hist,* LVII(1959):305–330.

9 TREAT, Victor Hugo. "Migration into Louisiana, 1834–1880." Doctoral dissertation, University of Texas, 1967.

5. The Negro

(For slavery, see 85.1–87.18.)

10 ANGLE, Paul M. "The Illinois Black Laws." *Chi Hist,* VIII(1967):65–75.

11 BELL, Howard H. "Expression of Negro Militancy in the North, 1840–1860." *J Neg Hist,* XLV(1960):11–20.

12 DAVIS, Edwin Adams, and William Ransom HOGAN. *The Barber of Natchez.* Baton Rouge, 1954. (See 52.16.)

13 ENGLAND, J. Merton. "The Free Negro in Ante-Bellum Tennessee." *J S Hist,* IX(1943):37–58.

14 FISCHER, Roger A. "Racial Segregation in Ante Bellum New Orleans." *Am Hist Rev,* LXXIV(1969):926–937.

15 FISCHER, Roger A. "The Segregation Struggle in Louisiana, 1850–1890." Doctoral dissertation, Tulane University, 1967.

16 FRANKLIN, John Hope. *The Free Negro in North Carolina, 1790–1860.* Chapel Hill, N.C., 1943.

17 FRANKLIN, John Hope. *From Slavery to Freedom: A History of American Negroes.* 3rd ed. New York, 1967.†

18 FURNAS, Joseph C. *Goodbye to Uncle Tom.* New York, 1956.†

19 GARVIN, Russell. "The Free Negro in Florida before the Civil War." *Fla Hist Q,* XLVI(1967):1–18.

20 JACKSON, Luther Porter. *Free Negro Labor and Property Holding in Virginia, 1830–1860.* New York, 1942.

21 KAPLAN, Sidney. "Herman Melville and the American National Sin." *J Neg Hist,* XLI(1956):311–338. Repr. in Seymour L. Gross and John Edward Hardy, eds., *Images of the Negro in American Literature.* Chicago, 1966.

1 LITWACK, Leon F. *North of Slavery: The Negro in the Free States, 1790–1860.* Chicago, 1961.†

2 MEIER, August, and Elliot M. RUDWICK. *From Plantation to Ghetto: An Interpretative History of American Negroes.* New York, 1966.

3 QUARLES, Benjamin. *Black Abolitionists.* New York, 1969.

4 QUARLES, Benjamin. *Frederick Douglass.* Washington, 1948.

5 REINDERS, Robert C. "The Free Negro in the New Orleans Economy, 1850–1860." *La Hist,* VI(1955):273–285.

6 STANTON, William. *The Leopard's Spots: Scientific Attitudes toward Race in America, 1815–59.* Chicago, 1960.†

7 THORNBROUGH, Emma Lou. *The Negro in Indiana.* Indianapolis, 1957.

8 WESLEY, Charles H. "The Participation of Negroes in Anti-Slavery Political Parties." *J Neg Hist,* XXIX(1944):32–74.

9 WOODSON, Carter G. *The Education of the Negro Prior to 1861.* New York, 1915.

6. *Family, Home, and Recreation*

10 BETTS, John Rickards. "The Technological Revolution and the Rise of Sport, 1850–1900." *Miss Val Hist Rev,* XL(1953):231–256.

11 BLAKE, Nelson M. *The Road to Reno: A History of Divorce in the United States.* New York, 1962.

12 CALHOUN, Arthur W. *A Social History of the American Family.* 3 vols. Cleveland, 1917–1919. (Particularly, Vol. II.)

13 DULLES, Foster Rhea. *America Learns to Play: A History of Popular Recreation, 1607–1940.* New York, 1940.†

14 ESAREY, Logan. *The Indiana Home.* Crawfordsville, Ind., 1947.

15 HERVEY, John. *Racing in America.* 2 vols. New York, 1944.

16 HOGAN, William Ransom. "Amusements in the Republic of Texas." *J S Hist,* III(1937):397–421.

17 HOWELLS, William Dean. *Years of My Youth.* New York, 1916.

18 KROUT, John Allen. *Annals of American Sport.* New Haven, Conn., 1929. (Vol. XV in the pictorial series, "The Pageant of America.")

19 LYNES, Russell. *The Domesticated Americans.* New York, 1963.

20 LYNN, Robert A. "Installment Credit before 1870." See 43.12.

21 MC CLELLAN, Elisabeth. *History of American Costume, 1607–1870.* New York, 1937. (First published in 1904.)

22 MANCHESTER, Herbert. *Four Centuries of Sport in America, 1490–1890.* New York, 1931.

23 MARTIN, Edgar W. *The Standard of Living in 1860.* See 39.9.

24 RILEY, Glenda Lou Gates. "From Chattel to Challenger: The Changing Image of the American Woman, 1828–1848." Doctoral dissertation, Ohio State University, 1967.

1 ROGERS, Meyric R. *American Interior Design: The Traditions and Development of Domestic Design from Colonial Times to the Present.* New York, 1947.

2 TAYLOR, William R., and Christopher LASCH. "Two 'Kindred Spirits': Sorority and Family in New England, 1839–1846." *N Eng Q*, XXXVI(1963): 23–41.

3 WELTER, Barbara. "The Cult of True Womanhood, 1820–1860." *Am Q*, XVIII(1966):151–174.

4 WISHY, Bernard. *The Child and the Republic: The Dawn of Modern American Child Nurture.* Philadelphia, 1968.

7. Health and Medicine

5 BONNER, Thomas N. *Medicine in Chicago, 1850–1950.* Madison, Wis., 1957.

6 CARRIGAN, Jo Ann. "Yellow Fever in New Orleans, 1853: Abstractions and Realities." *J S Hist*, XXV(1959):339–355.

7 DAIN, Norman. "Insanity: Changing Concepts in the United States, 1789–1865." Doctoral dissertation, Columbia University, 1961.

8 DUFFY, John. "Medical Practice in the Ante Bellum South." *J S Hist*, XXV(1959):53–72.

9 DUFFY, John, ed. *The Rudolph Matas History of Medicine in Louisiana.* 2 vols. Baton Rouge, 1958–1962. (Particularly, Vol. II.)

10 FLEXNER, James Thomas. *Doctors on Horseback: Pioneers of American Medicine.* Garden City, N.Y., 1939.

11 FÜLÖP-MILLER, René. *Triumph over Pain.* Trans. by Eden and Cedar Paul. New York, 1938. (On W. T. G. Morton and the discovery of anesthesia.)

12 GILLSON, Gordon. "Louisiana, Pioneer in Public Health." *La Hist*, IV(1963):207–232.

13 GROB, Gerald N. *The State and the Mentally Ill: A History of Worcester State Hospital in Massachusetts, 1830–1920.* Chapel Hill, N.C., 1966.

14 GROH, George W. *Gold Fever . . . the Art of Healing (So-Called) during the California Gold Rush.* New York, 1966.

15 HARRIS, Seale. *Woman's Surgeon: The Life Story of J. Marion Sims.* New York, 1950. (The "father of gynecology.")

16 HARSTAD, Peter T. "Health in the Upper Mississippi River Valley, 1820 to 1861." Doctoral dissertation, University of Wisconsin, 1963.

17 JONES, Billy M. *Health-Seekers in the Southwest, 1817–1900.* Norman, Okla., 1967.

18 KETT, Joseph F. *The Formation of the American Medical Profession: The Role of Institutions, 1780–1860.* New Haven, Conn., 1968.

19 MITCHELL, Martha Carolyn. "Health and the Medical Profession in the Lower South, 1845–1860." *J S Hist*, X(1944):424–446.

1   NORWOOD, William Frederick. *Medical Education in the United States before the Civil War*. Philadelphia, 1944. (School-by-school treatment.)

2   PACKARD, Francis R. *History of Medicine in the United States*. Rev. ed. 2 vols. New York, 1931. (First published in 1901.)

3   PICKARD, Madge E., and R. Carlyle BULEY. *The Midwest Pioneer, His Ills, Cures, and Doctors*. Crawfordsville, Ind., 1945.

4   ROBINSON, Victor. *Victory over Pain: A History of Anesthesia*. New York, 1946.

5   ROSENBERG, Charles E. "The American Medical Profession: Mid-Nineteenth Century." *Mid-Am*, XLIV(1962):163–171.

6   ROSENBERG, Charles E. *The Cholera Years: The United States in 1832, 1849, and 1866*. Chicago, 1962.†

7   ROSS, Ishbel. *Child of Destiny: The Life Story of the First Woman Doctor*. New York, 1949. (Elizabeth Blackwell.)

8   SHAFER, Henry Burnell. *The American Medical Profession, 1783 to 1850*. New York, 1936.

9   SHRYOCK, Richard Harrison. *Medicine and Society in America, 1660–1860*. New York, 1960. (Good background, but thin on period 1840–1860.)

8. Education

A. General

10   BROWN, Elmer E. *The Making of Our Middle Schools: An Account of the Development of Secondary Education in the United States*. New York, 1903.

11   BURNS, James A. *The Growth and Development of the Catholic School System in the United States*. New York, 1912.

12   BUTTS, R. Freeman, and Lawrence A. CREMIN. *A History of Education in American Culture*. New York, 1953.

13   CREMIN, Lawrence A. *The American Common School: An Historic Conception*. New York, 1951.

14   CUBBERLEY, Ellwood P. *Public Education in the United States*. Rev. ed. Boston, 1934.

15   CURTI, Merle. *The Social Ideas of American Educators*. New York, 1935.

16   WELTER, Rush. *Popular Education and Democratic Thought in America*. New York, 1962.†

17   WOODY, Thomas. *A History of Women's Education in the United States*. 2 vols. New York, 1929. (Topically arranged.)

B. Special Studies

18   ATHERTON, Lewis. "Mercantile Education in the Ante-Bellum South." *Miss Val Hist Rev*, XXXIX(1953):623–640.

1 BODE, Carl. *The American Lyceum, Town Meeting of the Mind.* New York, 1956.

2 CALLCOTT, George H. "History Enters the Schools." *Am Q*, XI(1959): 470–483.

3 CULVER, Raymond B. *Horace Mann and Religion in the Massachusetts Public Schools.* New Haven, Conn., 1929.

4 EBY, Frederick. *The Development of Education in Texas.* New York, 1925.

5 ELSON, Ruth Miller. *Guardians of Tradition: American Schoolbooks of the Nineteenth Century.* Lincoln, Neb., 1964.

6 JORGENSON, Lloyd P. *The Founding of Public Education in Wisconsin.* Madison, Wis., 1956.

7 KATZ, Michael. *The Irony of Early School Reform: Educational Innovation in Mid-Nineteenth Century Massachusetts.* Cambridge, Mass., 1968.

8 LANNIE, Vincent P. *Public Money and Parochial Education: Bishop Hughes, Governor Seward, and the New York School Controversy.* Cleveland, 1968. (For an extended debate between Lannie and John W. Pratt, see *N Y Hist*, XLII(1961):351–364; *Hist Ed Q*, IV(1964):181–192; V(1965):110–119; VI(1966):52–71.)

9 MESSERLI, Jonathan C. "Localism and State Control in Horace Mann's Reform of the Common Schools." *Am Q*, XVII(1965):104–118.

10 MINNICH, Harvey C. *William Holmes McGuffey and His Readers.* New York, 1936.

11 MOSIER, Richard D. *Making the American Mind: Social and Moral Ideas in the McGuffey Readers.* New York, 1947.

12 NIETZ, John A. *The Evolution of American Secondary School Textbooks.* Rutland, Vt., 1966.

13 PAWA, Jay Marvin. "The Attitude of Labor Organizations in New York State toward Public Education, 1829–1890." Doctoral dissertation, Columbia University, 1964.

14 THARP, Louise Hall. *Until Victory: Horace Mann and Mary Peabody.* Boston, 1953.

15 WOODSON, Carter G. *The Education of the Negro* . . . . See 57.9.

C. *Higher Education*

16 BRUCE, Philip Alexander. *History of the University of Virginia, 1819–1919.* 5 vols. New York, 1920–1922. (Particularly, Vol. III.)

17 CALKINS, Earnest Elmo. *They Broke the Prairie.* See 7.12.

18 CARRIEL, Mary Turner. *The Life of Jonathan Baldwin Turner.* Urbana, Ill., 1961. (Advocate of agricultural education.)

19 COLE, Arthur Charles. *A Hundred Years of Mount Holyoke College.* New Haven, Conn., 1940.

20 COULTER, E. Merton. *College Life in the Old South.* New York, 1928.

1 CURTI, Merle, and Vernon CARSTENSEN. *The University of Wisconsin: A History, 1848–1925*. 2 vols. Madison, Wis., 1949.

2 FLETCHER, Robert Samuel. *A History of Oberlin College from Its Foundation through the Civil War*. 2 vols. Oberlin, Ohio, 1943.

3 GODBOLD, Albea. *The Church College of the Old South*. Durham, N.C., 1944.

4 HOLLIS, Daniel Walker. *University of South Carolina*. 2 vols. Columbia, S.C., 1951–1956.

5 PERRY, Charles M. *Henry Philip Tappan, Philosopher and University President*. Ann Arbor, Mich., 1933.

6 RICHARDSON, Leon Burr. *History of Dartmouth College*. 2 vols. Hanover, N.H., 1932.

7 RUDOLPH, Frederick. *The American College and University*. New York, 1962.†

8 RUDOLPH, Frederick. *Mark Hopkins and the Log: Williams College, 1836–1872*. New Haven, Conn., 1956.

9 SELLERS, James B. *History of the University of Alabama, 1818–1902*. University, Ala., 1953.

10 STEPHENS, Frank F. *A History of the University of Missouri*. Columbia, Mo., 1962.

11 TEWKSBURY, Donald G. *The Founding of American Colleges and Universities before the Civil War*. New York, 1932.

12 WHITE, Andrew Dickson. *Autobiography*. 2 vols. New York, 1905. (First president of Cornell.)

13 WOODBURN, James Albert. *History of Indiana University, 1820–1902*. Bloomington, Ind., 1940.

9. Religion

A. General

14 DRUMMOND, Andrew Landale. *Story of American Protestantism*. Boston, 1950.

15 ELLIS, John Tracy. *American Catholicism*. Chicago, 1956.†

16 GAUSTAD, Edwin Scott. *A Religious History of America*. New York, 1966.

17 HUDSON, Winthrop S. *Religion in America*. New York, 1965.†

18 LATOURETTE, Kenneth Scott. *Christianity in a Revolutionary Age*. 5 vols. New York, 1958–1962. (Particularly, Vol. III.)

19 LATOURETTE, Kenneth Scott. *A History of the Expansion of Christianity*. 7 vols. New York, 1937–1945. (Particularly, Vol. IV.)

20 MEAD, Sidney E. *The Lively Experiment: The Shaping of Christianity in America*. New York, 1963.

21 OLMSTEAD, Clifton E. *History of Religion in the United States*. Englewood Cliffs, N.J., 1960.

1 POSEY, Walter Brownlow. *Frontier Mission: A History of Religion West of the Southern Appalachians to 1861.* Lexington, Ky., 1966.

2 STEPHENSON, George M. *The Puritan Heritage.* New York, 1952.

3 SWEET, William Warren. *The Story of Religion in America.* New York, 1930.

B. Special Studies

4 CLARK, Joseph B. *Leavening the Nation: The Story of American Home Missions.* New York, 1903.

5 COX, Harold E. " 'Daily Except Sunday': Blue Laws and the Operation of Philadelphia Horsecars." *Bus Hist Rev,* XXXIX(1965):228–242. (A sabbatarian controversy in 1859.)

6 CROSS, Whitney Rogers. *The Burned-Over District: The Social and Intellectual History of Enthusiastic Religion in Western New York, 1800–1850.* Ithaca, N.Y., 1950.

7 GOODYKOONTZ, Colin Brummitt. *Home Missions on the American Frontier, with Particular Reference to the American Home Missionary Society.* Caldwell, Idaho, 1939.

8 GREEN, Fletcher M. "Northern Missionary Activities in the South, 1846–1861." *J S Hist,* XXI(1955):147–172.

9 HOPKINS, Charles Howard. *History of the Y.M.C.A. in North America.* New York, 1951.

10 HOUF, Walter Ralph. "The Protestant Church in the Rural Midwestern Community, 1820–1870." Doctoral dissertation, University of Missouri, 1967.

11 HUTCHISON, William R. *The Transcendentalist Ministers: Church Reform in the New England Renaissance.* New Haven, Conn., 1959.†

12 KORN, Bertram Wallace. *The American Reaction to the Mortara Case, 1858–1859.* Cincinnati, 1957. (Abduction of a Jewish child by Catholic authorities in Italy.)

13 LOUD, Grover C. *Evangelized America.* New York, 1928.

14 NIEBUHR, H. Richard. *The Social Sources of Denominationalism.* See 54.11.

15 POSEY, Walter Brownlow. *Religious Strife on the Southern Frontier.* Baton Rouge, 1965.

16 WOODSON, Carter G. *The History of the Negro Church.* Washington, 1921.

C. Denominations, Sects, and Cults

17 BUCKE, Emory Stevens, ed. *The History of American Methodism.* 3 vols. New York, 1964. (Particularly, Vol. II.)

18 GARRISON, Winfred Ernest, and Alfred T. DE GROOT. *The Disciples of Christ: A History.* St Louis, 1948.

1 MANROSS, William Wilson. *A History of the American Episcopal Church.* Rev. ed. New York, 1950.

2 MELCHER, Marguerite. *The Shaker Adventure.* Princeton, 1941.

3 NICHOL, Francis D. *The Midnight Cry.* Washington, 1944. (Millerites, sympathetic.)

4 PODMORE, Frank. *Modern Spiritualism: A History and a Criticism.* 2 vols New York, 1902.

5 POST, Albert. *Popular Free Thought in America, 1825–1850.* New York, 1943.

6 ROBERTS, B. H. . . . *Latter-day Saints.* See 22.14.

7 SEARS, Clara E. *Days of Delusion.* Boston, 1924. (Millerites, critical.)

8 THOMPSON, Ernest Trice. *Presbyterians in the South, Volume One: 1607–1861.* Richmond, 1963.

9 TORBET, Robert G. *A History of the Baptists.* Philadelphia, 1950.

10 WENTZ, Abdel Ross. *A Basic History of Lutheranism in America.* Philadelphia, 1955.

D. Religion and Society

11 BILLINGTON, Ray Allen. *The Protestant Crusade.* See 54.1.

12 BODO, John R. *The Protestant Clergy and Public Issues, 1812–1848.* Princeton, 1954.

13 COLE, Charles C., Jr. *The Social Ideas of the Northern Evangelists, 1826–1860.* New York, 1954.

14 DRAKE, Thomas E. *Quakers and Slavery in America.* New Haven, Conn., 1950.

15 ELLSWORTH, Clayton Sumner. "The American Churches and the Mexican War." See 18.17.

16 ENGELDER, Conrad James. "The Churches and Slavery: A Study of the Attitudes toward Slavery of the Major Protestant Denominations." Doctoral dissertation, University of Michigan, 1964.

17 FORTENBAUGH, Robert. "American Lutheran Synods and Slavery, 1830–1860." *J Rel*, XIII(1933):72–92.

18 HOWARD, Victor B. "The Anti-Slavery Movement in the Presbyterian Church, 1835–1861." Doctoral dissertation, Ohio State University, 1961.

19 MATHEWS, Donald G. *Slavery and Methodism: A Chapter in American Morality, 1780–1845.* Princeton, 1965.

20 MAY, Henry F. *Protestant Churches and Industrial America.* New York, 1949. (Part I: "The Conservative Mold, 1828–1861.")

21 POWELL, Milton Bryan. "The Abolitionist Controversy in the Methodist Episcopal Church, 1840–1864." Doctoral dissertation, University of Iowa, 1963.

1 PURIFOY, Lewis McCarroll, Jr. "The Methodist Episcopal Church, South, and Slavery, 1844–1865." Doctoral dissertation, University of North Carolina, 1965.

2 PURIFOY, Lewis McCarroll, Jr. "The Southern Methodist Church and the Proslavery Argument." *J S Hist*, XXXII(1966):325–341.

3 RICE, Madeleine Hooke. *American Catholic Opinion in the Slavery Controversy*. New York, 1943.

4 SMITH, Timothy L. *Revivalism and Social Reform in Mid-Nineteenth-Century America*. New York, 1957.†

5 SWANEY, Charles Baumer. *Episcopal Methodism and Slavery, with Sidelights on Ecclesiastical Politics*. Boston, 1926.

E. Biography
(Listed alphabetically by subject)

6 HIBBEN, Paxton. *Henry Ward Beecher: An American Portrait*. New York, 1927.

7 CROSS, Barbara M. *Horace Bushnell, Minister to a Changing America*. Chicago, 1958.

8 CULVER, Raymond B. *Horace Mann and Religion* . . . . See 60.3.

9 COMMAGER, Henry Steele. *Theodore Parker*. Boston, 1936.

10 SPITZ, Lewis W. *Life in Two Worlds: A Biography of William Sihler*. St. Louis, 1968.

11 MEAD, Sidney E. *Nathaniel William Taylor, 1786–1858, a Connecticut Liberal*. Chicago, 1942.

12 KNOX, Israel. *Rabbi in America: The Story of Isaac M. Wise*. Boston, 1957.

10. Social Experiment and Reform
(For antislavery, see 87.19–89.16.)

A. General

13 BREMNER, Robert H. *American Philanthropy*. Chicago, 1960.†

14 CALVERTON, Victor Francis. *Where Angels Dared to Tread*. Indianapolis 1941.

15 DAVIS, David Brion, ed. *Ante-Bellum Reform*. New York, 1967.† (Anthology of essays and passages from books.)

16 EGBERT, Donald Drew, and Stow PERSONS. *Socialism* . . . . See 52.2.

17 GRIFFIN, Clifford S. *The Ferment of Reform, 1830–1860*. New York, 1967.†

18 GRIFFIN, Clifford S. *Their Brother's Keepers: Moral Stewardship in the United States, 1800–1865*. New Brunswick, N.J., 1960.

19 HOLLOWAY, Mark. *Heavens on Earth: Utopian Communities in America, 1680–1880*. London, 1951.

1 NORDHOFF, Charles. *The Communistic Societies of the United States.* New York, 1875.

2 SELDES, Gilbert. *The Stammering Century.* New York, 1928.

3 SMITH, Timothy L. *Revivalism and Social Reform* .... See 64.4.

4 THOMAS, John L. "Romantic Reform in America, 1815–1865." *Am Q,* XVII(1965):656–681. (Repr. without footnotes in Davis book, see 64.15.

5 WEBBER, Everett. *Escape to Utopia: The Communal Movement in America.* New York, 1959.

B. Special Studies

6 BOUDREAUX, Julianna Liles. "A History of Philanthropy in New Orleans, 1835–1862." Doctoral dissertation, Tulane University, 1961.

7 BREMNER, Robert H. *From the Depths: The Discovery of Poverty in the United States.* New York, 1956.†

8 BROCK, Peter. *Radical Pacifists in Antebellum America.* Princeton, 1968.† (Selected portions from the author's longer work, *Pacifism in America.* Princeton, 1968.)

9 CHRISTMAN, Henry. *Tin Horns and Calico.* New York, 1945.† (Anti-rent uprising in New York, 1839–1846.)

10 CURTI, Merle. *The American Peace Crusade, 1815–1860.* Durham, N.C., 1929.

11 CURTIS, Edith Roelker. *A Season in Utopia: The Story of Brook Farm.* New York, 1961.

12 DAVIS, David Brion. "The Movement to Abolish Capital Punishment in America, 1787–1861." *Am Hist Rev,* LXIII(1957):23–46.

13 FLEXNER, Eleanor. *A Century of Struggle: The Woman's Rights Movement in the United States.* Cambridge, Mass., 1959.

14 GUSFIELD, Joseph R. *Symbolic Crusade: Status Politics and the American Temperance Movement.* Urbana, Ill., 1963.

15 KROUT, John Allen. *The Origins of Prohibition.* New York, 1925.

16 LUCID, Robert F. "*Two Years Before the Mast* as Propaganda." *Am Q,* XII(1960):392–403.

17 LUDLUM, David M. *Social Ferment in Vermont, 1791–1850.* New York, 1939.

18 MC BEE, Alice Eaton, 2nd. *From Utopia to Florence: The Story of a Transcendentalist Community in Northampton, Mass., 1830–1852. Stud Hist* (Smith), XXXII. Northampton, Mass., 1947.

19 MELCHER, Marguerite. *The Shaker Adventure.* See 63.2.

20 PEARSON, C. C., and J. Edwin HENDRICKS. *Liquor and Anti-Liquor in Virginia, 1619–1919.* Durham, N.C., 1967.

21 RIEGEL, Robert Edgar. *American Feminists.* Lawrence, Kan., 1963.†

22 SWIFT, Lindsay. *Brook Farm: Its Members, Scholars, and Visitors.* New York, 1900.

C. Biography
(Listed alphabetically by subject)

1 ANTHONY, Katharine. *Susan B. Anthony: Her Personal History and Her Era*. Garden City, N.Y., 1954.

2 HARPER, Ida H. *The Life and Work of Susan B. Anthony*. 3 vols. Indianapolis, 1898–1908. (Particularly, Vol. I.)

3 TOLIS, Peter. *Elihu Burritt: Crusader for Brotherhood*. Hamden, Conn., 1968.

4 BROOKS, Gladys. *Three Wise Virgins*. New York, 1957. (Dorothea Dix, Elizabeth Peabody, and Catharine Sedgwick.)

5 MARSHALL, Helen E. *Dorothea Dix, Forgotten Samaritan*. Chapel Hill, N.C., 1937.

6 SCHWARTZ, Harold. *Samuel Gridley Howe, Social Reformer, 1801–1876*. Cambridge, Mass., 1956.

7 CROMWELL, Otelia. *Lucretia Mott*. Cambridge, Mass., 1958.

8 PARKER, Robert Allerton. *A Yankee Saint: John Humphrey Noyes and the Oneida Community*. New York, 1935.

9 LEOPOLD, Richard William. *Robert Dale Owen: A Biography*. Cambridge, Mass., 1940.

10 CROWE, Charles. *George Ripley: Transcendentalist and Utopian Socialist*. Athens, Ga., 1967.

11 COMMAGER, Henry Steele. *Theodore Parker*. See 64.9.

12 LUTZ, Alma. *Created Equal: A Biography of Elizabeth Cady Stanton*. New York, 1940.

13 STANTON, Theodore, and Harriet Stanton BLATCH, eds. *Elizabeth Cady Stanton, as Revealed in Her Letters, Diary and Reminiscences*. 2 vols. New York, 1922.

14 HAYS, Elinor Rice. *Morning Star: A Biography of Lucy Stone, 1812–1893*. New York, 1961.

15 THORP, Margaret. *Female Persuasion: Six Strong-Minded Women*. New Haven, Conn., 1949.

VI. Art and Thought

1. Bibliography

16 BLANCK, Jacob. *Bibliography of American Literature*. 5 vols. New Haven, Conn., 1955–1968. (In progress, completed alphabetically through "Longfellow.")

17 CARPENTER, Frederic Ives. *Emerson Handbook*. New York, 1953.

18 CHAMBERLIN, Mary W. *Guide to Art Reference Books*. Chicago, 1959.

19 HARDING, Walter. *A Thoreau Handbook*. New York, 1959.†

1 HOLMAN, C. Hugh. *The American Novel through Henry James*. New York, 1966.† (Goldentree Bibliography.)

2 LEARY, Lewis. *Articles on American Literature, 1900–1950*. Durham, N.C. 1954.

3 MEISEL, Max. *A Bibliography of American Natural History: The Pioneer, Century, 1769–1865*. 3 vols. Brooklyn, 1924–1929.

4 ROOS, Frank J., Jr. *Writings on Early American Architecture*. Columbus, Ohio, 1943. (Eastern half of United States to 1860.)

5 STOVALL, Floyd, ed. *Eight American Authors: A Review of Research and Criticism*. New York, 1963.† (Includes Poe, Emerson, Hawthorne, Thoreau, Melville, and Whitman.)

2. Selected Source Materials

6 BLAU, Joseph L., ed. *American Philosophic Addresses, 1700–1900*. New York, 1946.

7 CURTI, Merle, ed. *The Learned Blacksmith: The Letters and Journals of Elihu Burritt*. New York, 1937.

8 FITZHUGH, George. *Cannibals All! or Slaves without Masters*. Ed. by C. Vann Woodward. Cambridge, Mass., 1960.† (First published in 1857.)

9 FITZHUGH, George. *Sociology for the South; or, the Failure of Free Society*. Richmond, 1854.

10 FOGLE, Richard Harter, ed. *The Romantic Movement in American Writing*. New York, 1966.† (Anthology.)

11 GRAY, Jane Loring, ed. *Letters of Asa Gray*. 2 vols. Boston, 1893.

12 HARDING, Walter, and Carl BODE, eds. *The Correspondence of Henry David Thoreau*. New York, 1958.

13 HERBER, Elmer Charles, ed. *Correspondence between Spencer Fullerton Baird and Louis Agassiz—Two Pioneer American Naturalists*. Washington, 1963.

14 LEYDA, Jay. *The Melville Log: A Documentary Life of Herman Melville, 1819–1891*. 2 vols. New York, 1951.

15 MILLER, Perry, ed. *The Transcendentalists: An Anthology*. Cambridge, Mass., 1950.

16 MELTZER, Milton, ed. *Thoreau: People, Principles, and Politics*. New York, 1963.† (Selection of Thoreau's writings on man and society.)

17 MOODY, Richard, ed. *Dramas from the American Theater, 1762–1909*. Cleveland, 1966.

18 MOSES, Montrose J., ed. *Representative Plays by American Dramatists from 1765 to the Present Day*. 3 vols. New York, 1918–1925.

19 SMALL, Harold A., ed. *Form and Function: Remarks on Art by Horatio Greenough*. Berkeley, 1947.

1 WAINRIGHT, Nicholas B., ed. *A Philadelphia Perspective: The Diary of Sidney George Fisher . . . 1834–1871.* Philadelphia, 1967.

2 WARFEL, Harry R., Ralph Henry GABRIEL, and Stanley T. WILLIAMS, eds. *The American Mind: Selections from the Literature of the United States.* New York, 1937.

3 WILSON, Edmund, ed. *The Shock of Recognition: The Development of Literature in the United States Recorded by the Men Who Made It.* Garden City, N.Y., 1943. (Contemporary criticism.)

3. General Studies

4 BARTLETT, Irving H. *The American Mind in the Mid-Nineteenth Century.* New York, 1967.†

5 BOAS, George, ed. *Romanticism in America.* Baltimore, 1940. (Symposium.)

6 BODE, Carl. *The Anatomy of American Popular Culture, 1840–1861.* Berkeley, 1959.

7 CALLOW, James T. *Kindred Spirits: Knickerbocker Writers and American Artists, 1807–1855.* Chapel Hill, N.C., 1967.

8 CURTI, Merle. *The Growth of American Thought.* 3rd ed. New York, 1964. (The most comprehensive study, first published in 1943.)

9 EATON, Clement. *The Mind of the Old South.* Baton Rouge, 1964.†

10 EKIRCH, Arthur Alphonse, Jr. *The Idea of Progress in America, 1815–1860.* New York, 1944.

11 GABRIEL, Ralph Henry. *The Course of American Democratic Thought.* New York, 1940.

12 JONES, Howard Mumford. "The Influence of European Ideas in Nineteenth Century America." *Am Lit*, VII(1935):241–273.

13 KOUWENHOVEN, John A. *Made in America.* See 40.12.

14 LYNES, Russell. *The Taste-Makers.* New York, 1954.

15 MILLER, Perry. *The Life of the Mind in America.* See 27.15.

16 MILLER, Perry. *Nature's Nation.* Cambridge, Mass., 1967. (Essays.)

17 MOSIER, Richard D. *The American Temper: Patterns of Our Intellectual Heritage.* Berkeley, 1952.

18 PARRINGTON, Vernon Louis. *The Romantic Revolution in America, 1800–1860.* New York, 1927.† (Vol. II of his *Main Currents in American Thought.*)

19 PERSONS, Stow. *American Minds: A History of Ideas.* New York, 1958.

20 ROURKE, Constance Mayfield. *Trumpets of Jubilee.* New York, 1927.

21 SOMKIN, Fred. *Unquiet Eagle: Memory and Desire in the Idea of American Freedom, 1815–1860.* Ithaca, N.Y., 1967.

1 STEIN, Roger B. *John Ruskin and Aesthetic Thought in America, 1840–1900.* Cambridge, Mass., 1967.

2 WISH, Harvey. *Society and Thought in Early America.* See 53.16.

4. *Science*

(For technology, see 40.1–41.5; for medicine, see 58.5–59.9.)

3 COULSON, Thomas. *Joseph Henry: His Life and Work.* Princeton, 1950. (Physicist.)

4 DALL, William Healey. *Spencer Fullerton Baird.* Philadelphia, 1915. (Zoologist.)

5 DANIELS, George H. "The Process of Professionalization in American Science: The Emergent Period, 1820–1860." *Isis,* LVIII(1967):151–166.

6 DUPREE, A. Hunter. *Science in the Federal Government.* Cambridge, Mass., 1957.

7 FLEMING, Donald. *John William Draper and the Religion of Science.* Philadelphia, 1950.

8 FULTON, John F., and Elizabeth H. THOMSON. *Benjamin Silliman, 1779–1864.* New York, 1947. (Chemist, geologist.)

9 GILMAN, Daniel Coit. *The Life of James Dwight Dana.* New York, 1899. (Geologist.)

10 JOHNSON, Thomas Cary, Jr. *Scientific Interests in the Old South.* New York, 1936.

11 JORDAN, David Starr, ed. *Leading American Men of Science.* New York, 1910.

12 LURIE, Edward. *Louis Agassiz: A Life in Science.* Chicago, 1960.†

13 ODGERS, Merle M. *Alexander Dallas Bache, Scientist and Educator, 1806–1867.* Philadelphia, 1947. (Physicist.)

14 PICKARD, Madge E. "Government and Science in the United States: Historical Backgrounds." *J Hist Med,* I(1946):254–289, 446–481. (Second installment is on founding of Smithsonian Institution.)

15 RODGERS, Andrew Denny. *John Torrey: A Story of North American Botany.* Princeton, 1942.

16 STANTON, William. *The Leopard's Spots.* See 57.6.

17 STRUIK, Dirk J. *Yankee Science in the Making.* Boston, 1948.

18 SYDNOR, Charles S. "State Geological Surveys in the Old South." *American Studies in Honor of William Kenneth Boyd.* Ed. by David Kelly Jackson Durham, N.C., 1940.

19 WILLIAMS, Frances Leigh. *Matthew Fontaine Maury, Scientist of the Sea.* New Brunswick, N.J., 1963.

20 YOUMANS, William Jay, ed. *Pioneers of Science in America.* New York, 1896.

5. *Philosophy, Social Thought, and Scholarship*

A. *General*

1 BERNARD, L. L. and Jessie B. *The Origins of American Sociology.* New York, 1943.

2 BLAU, Joseph L. *Men and Movements in American Philosophy.* Englewood Cliffs, N.J., 1952.

3 DORFMAN, Joseph. *The Economic Mind . . . .* See 39.5.

4 LEVIN, David. *History as Romantic Art: Bancroft, Prescott, Motley, and Parkman.* Stanford, 1959.†

5 MERRIAM, Charles E. *A History of American Political Theories.* New York, 1903.

6 SCHNEIDER, Herbert W. *A History of American Philosophy.* New York, 1946.†

7 VAN TASSEL, David D. *Recording America's Past: An Interpretation of the Development of Historical Studies in America, 1607–1884.* Chicago, 1960.

B. *Special Studies*

8 COLE, Charles C., Jr. *The Social Ideas of . . . Evangelists.* See 63.13.

9 COOKE, John White. "Some Aspects of the Concept of the Free Individual in the United States, 1800–1860." Doctoral dissertation, Vanderbilt University, 1967.

10 CURTI, Merle. "The Great Mr. Locke: America's Philosopher, 1783–1861." *Hunt Lib Bull*, XI(April, 1937):107–151.

11 FROTHINGHAM, Octavius Brooks. *Transcendentalism in New England.* New York, 1876.†

12 GODDARD, Harold Clarke. *Studies in New England Transcendentalism.* New York, 1908.

13 MADDEN, Edward H. *Civil Disobedience and Moral Law in Nineteenth-Century American Philosophy.* Seattle, 1968.

14 MARSHALL, Philip Clark. "The Social Ideas of American Historians, 1815–1865." Doctoral dissertation, Rutgers University, 1963.

15 MARX, Leo. *The Machine in the Garden.* See 40.15.

16 NAGEL, Paul C. *One Nation Indivisible: The Union in American Thought, 1776–1861.* New York, 1964.

C. *Individuals*
(Listed alphabetically by subject)

17 GLICK, Wendell. "The Best Possible World of John Quincy Adams." *N Eng Q*, XXXVII(1964):3–17.

18 SCHLESINGER, Arthur M., Jr. *Orestes A. Brownson: A Pilgrim's Progress.* Boston, 1939.†

1 CURRENT, Richard N. *John C. Calhoun.* New York, 1963.†

2 FREEHLING, William W. "Spoilsmen and Interests in the Thought and Career of John C. Calhoun." *J Am Hist*, LII(1965):25–42. (Reprinted in 36.9.)

3 LERNER, Ralph. "Calhoun's New Science of Politics." *Am Pol Sci Rev*, LVII(1963):918–932. (Reprinted in 36.9.)

4 MERRIAM, Charles E. "The Political Philosophy of John C. Calhoun." *Studies in Southern History and Politics Inscribed to William Archibald Dunning.* New York, 1914.

5 SPAIN, August O. *The Politican Theory of John C. Calhoun.* New York, 1951.

6 LEIMAN, Melvin M. *Jacob N. Cardozo.* See 39.8.

7 GREEN, Arnold W. *Henry Charles Carey, Nineteenth-Century Sociologist.* Philadelphia, 1951.

8 HESSELTINE, William D. *Pioneer's Mission: The Story of Lyman Copeland Draper.* Madison, Wis., 1954. (Historian and collector.)

9 CHRISTY, Arthur. *The Orient in American Transcendentalism: A Study of Emerson, Thoreau, and Alcott.* New York, 1932.

10 NICOLOFF, Philip L. *Emerson on Race and History: An Examination of "English Traits."* New York, 1961.

11 PORTE, Joel. *Emerson and Thoreau, Transcendentalists in Conflict.* Middletown, Conn., 1965.

12 WHICHER, Stephen E. *Freedom and Fate: An Inner Life of Ralph Waldo Emerson.* Philadelphia, 1953.†

13 LEAVELLE, Arnaud B., and Thomas I. COOK. "George Fitzhugh and the Theory of American Conservatism." *J Pol*, VII(1945):145–168.

14 WISH, Harvey. *George Fitzhugh, Propagandist of the Old South.* Baton Rouge, 1943.

15 HALL, Lawrence Sargent. *Hawthorne, Critic of Society.* New Haven, Conn., 1944.

16 WARREN, Austin. *The Elder Henry James.* New York, 1934.

17 FREIDEL, Frank. *Francis Lieber, Nineteenth-Century Liberal.* Baton Rouge, 1947.

18 STERN, Bernhard J. *Lewis Henry Morgan, Social Evolutionist.* Chicago, 1931.

19 BEVERIDGE, Charles Eliot. "Frederick Law Olmsted: The Formative Years, 1822–1865." Doctoral dissertation, University of Wisconsin, 1966.

20 ROPER, Laura Wood. "Frederick Law Olmsted in the 'Literary Republic.' " *Miss Val Hist Rev*, XXXIX(1952):459–482.

21 WADE, Mason. *Francis Parkman, Heroic Historian.* New York, 1942.

22 TYACK, David B. *George Ticknor and the Boston Brahmins.* Cambridge, Mass., 1967.

6. *Literature*

A. *General*

1 BROOKS, Van Wyck. *The Flowering of New England, 1815–1865.* New York, 1936.†

2 BROOKS, Van Wyck. *The Times of Melville and Whitman.* New York, 1947.

3 CLARK, Harry H., ed. *Transitions in American Literary History.* Durham, N.C., 1953.

4 COWIE, Alexander. *The Rise of the American Novel.* New York, 1948.

5 FEIDELSON, Charles, Jr., and Paul BRODTKORB, Jr., eds. *Interpretations of American Literature.* New York, 1959.† (Anthology of scholarly essays.)

6 HART, James D. *The Popular Book: A History of America's Literary Taste.* New York, 1950.†

7 KAUL, A. N. *The American Vision: Actual and Ideal Society in Nineteenth-Century Fiction.* New Haven, Conn., 1963.

8 KREYMBORG, Alfred. *Our Singing Strength: An Outline of American Poetry, 1620–1930.* New York, 1929.

9 LEWIS, R. W. B. *The American Adam: Innocence, Tragedy and Tradition in the Nineteenth Century.* Chicago, 1955.†

10 MATTHIESSEN, F. O. *American Renaissance: Art and Expression in the Age of Emerson and Whitman.* New York, 1941.†

11 MILLER, Perry. *The Raven and the Whale: The War of Words and Wits in the Era of Poe and Melville.* New York, 1956.†

12 MOTT, Frank Luther. *Golden Multitudes: The Story of Best Sellers in the United States.* New York, 1947.

13 PATTEE, Fred Lewis. *The Feminine Fifties.* See 53.14.

14 SPILLER, Robert E., et al., eds. *Literary History of the United States.* 3rd ed. New York, 1963.

15 WELLEK, René. *A History of Modern Criticism, 1750–1950.* 4 vols. New Haven, Conn., 1955–1965. (Particularly, Vol. III.)

16 WILSON, Edmund. *Patriotic Gore: Studies in the Literature of the American Civil War.* New York, 1962.†

B. *Special Studies*

17 BLAIR, Walter. *Native American Humor.* New York, 1937.†

18 BROWN, Herbert Ross. *The Sentimental Novel in America, 1789–1860.* Durham, N.C., 1940.

19 DAVIS, David Brion. *Homicide in American Fiction, 1798–1860: A Study in Social Values.* Ithaca, N.Y., 1957.†

1 DUVALL, Severn. *"Uncle Tom's Cabin:* The Sinister Side of the Patriarchy." *N Eng Q*, XXXVI(1963):3–22. (Repr. in *Images of the Negro;* see 56.21.)

2 FOGLE, Richard Harter. "Organic Form in American Criticism, 1840–1870." *The Development of American Literary Criticism.* Ed. by Floyd Stovall. Chapel Hill, N.C., 1955

3 FUSSELL, Edwin S. *Frontier: American Literature and the American West.* Princeton, 1965.

4 HERRON, Ima Honaker. *The Small Town in American Literature.* New York, 1959.

5 HUBBELL, Jay B. "Literary Nationalism in the Old South." *American Studies in Honor of William Kenneth Boyd.* See 69.18.

6 HUBBELL, Jay B. *The South in American Literature, 1607–1900.* Durham, N.C., 1954.

7 LIEDEL, Donald Edward. "The Antislavery Novel, 1836–1861." Doctoral dissertation, University of Michigan, 1961.

8 PAPASHVILY, Helen Waite. *All the Happy Endings.* New York, 1956. (The domestic novel, by women and for women.)

9 PARKS, Edd Winfield. *Ante-Bellum Southern Literary Critics.* Athens, Ga., 1962.

10 PRITCHARD, John Paul. *Literary Wise Men of Gotham: Criticism in New York, 1815–1860.* Baton Rouge, 1963.

11 STAFFORD, John. *The Literary Criticism of "Young America": A Study in the Relationship of Politics and Literature, 1837–1850.* Berkeley, 1952.

C. Individuals
(Listed alphabetically by subject)

12 SHEPPARD, Odell. *Pedlar's Progress: The Life of Bronson Alcott.* Boston, 1937.

13 DAVIS, Curtis Carroll. *Chronicler of the Cavaliers: A Life of the Virginia Novelist, Dr. William A. Caruthers.* Richmond, 1953.

14 GROSSMAN, James. *James Fenimore Cooper.* New York, 1949.†

15 SPILLER, Robert E. *Fenimore Cooper, Critic of His Times.* New York, 1931.

16 RUSK, Ralph L. *The Life of Ralph Waldo Emerson.* New York, 1949.

17 WADE, Mason. *Margaret Fuller, Whetstone of Genius.* New York, 1940.

18 HOELTJE, Hubert H. *Inward Sky: The Mind and Heart of Nathaniel Hawthorne.* Durham, N.C., 1962.

19 STEWART, Randall. *Nathaniel Hawthorne: A Biography.* New Haven, Conn., 1948.†

20 HOWE, M. A. DeWolf. *Holmes of the Breakfast Table.* New York, 1939.

21 TILTON, Eleanor Marguerite. *Amiable Autocrat: A Biography of Dr. Oliver Wendell Holmes.* New York, 1947.

1   WILLIAMS, Stanley T. *The Life of Washington Irving.* 2 vols. New York, 1935.

2   BOHNER, Charles H. *John Pendleton Kennedy, Gentleman from Baltimore.* Baltimore, 1961.

3   WAGENKNECHT, Edward. *Longfellow: A Full-Length Portrait.* New York, 1955.

4   DUBERMAN, Martin. *James Russell Lowell.* Boston, 1966.

5   HOWARD, Leon. *Victorian Knight-Errant: A Study of the Early Literary Career of James Russell Lowell.* Berkeley, 1952.

6   ARVIN, Newton. *Herman Melville.* New York, 1950.

7   HEIMERT, Alan. "*Moby-Dick* and American Political Symbolism." *Am Q,* XV(1963):498–534.

8   HOWARD, Leon. *Herman Melville: A Biography.* Berkeley, 1951.

9   THARP, Louise Hall. *The Peabody Sisters of Salem.* Boston, 1950.

10 ALLEN, Hervey. *Israfel: The Life and Times of Edgar Allan Poe.* 2 vols. New York, 1929.

11 QUINN, Arthur H. *Edgar Allan Poe: A Critical Biography.* New York, 1941.

12 HIGHAM, John. "The Changing Loyalties of William Gilmore Simms." *J S Hist,* IX(1943):210–223.

13 WAKELYN, Jon Louis. "William Gilmore Simms: The Artist as Public Man, a Political Odyssey, 1830–1860." Doctoral dissertation, Rice University, 1966.

14 FOSTER, Charles H. *The Rungless Ladder: Harriet Beecher Stowe and New England Puritanism.* Durham, N.C., 1954.

15 WILSON, Forrest. *Crusader in Crinoline: The Life of Harriet Beecher Stowe.* Philadelphia, 1941.

16 KRUTCH, Joseph Wood. *Henry David Thoreau.* New York, 1948.†

17 PAUL, Sherman. *The Shores of America: Thoreau's Inward Exploration.* Urbana, Ill., 1958.

18 ALLEN, Gay W. *The Solitary Singer: A Critical Biography of Walt Whitman.* New York, 1955.

19 CANBY, Henry Seidel. *Walt Whitman, an American.* Boston, 1943.

20 MORDELL, Albert. *Quaker Militant: John Greenleaf Whittier.* Boston, 1933.

21 POLLARD, John A. *John Greenleaf Whittier, Friend of Man.* Boston, 1949.

7. The Fine Arts

A. General

22 LARKIN, Oliver W. *Art and Life in America.* New York, 1949.

23 MENDELOWITZ, Daniel M. *A History of American Art.* New York, 1960.

1   MILLER, Lillian B. *Patrons and Patriotism: The Encouragement of the Fine Arts in the United States, 1790–1860.* Chicago, 1966.

B.   Architecture

2   ANDREWS, Wayne. *Architecture, Ambition, and Americans.* New York, 1955.†

3   BONNER, James C. "Plantation Architecture of the Lower South on the Eve of the Civil War." *J S Hist*, XI(1945):370–388.

4   BURCHARD, James, and Albert BUSH-BROWN. *The Architecture of America: A Social and Cultural History.* Boston, 1966.

5   EARLY, James. *Romanticism and American Architecture.* New York, 1965.

6   FORMAN, Henry Chandlee. *The Architecture of the Old South: The Medieval Style, 1585–1850.* Cambridge, Mass., 1948.

7   GILCHRIST, Agnes Addison. *William Strickland, Architect and Engineer, 1788–1854.* Philadelphia, 1950.

8   GOWANS, Alan. *Images of American Living: Four Centuries of Architecture and Furniture as Cultural Expression.* New York, 1964.

9   HAMLIN, Talbot P. *Greek Revival Architecture in America.* New York, 1944.

10 KIRKER, Harold. *California's Architectural Frontier: Style and Tradition in the Nineteenth Century.* San Marino, Calif., 1960.

11 LANCASTER, Clay. *Back Streets and Pine Trees: The Work of John McMurtry, Nineteenth Century Architect Builder of Kentucky.* Lexington, Ky., 1956.

12 LANCASTER, Clay. "Italianism in American Architecture before 1860." *Am Q*, IV(1952):127–148.

C.   Painting and Sculpture

13 BARKER, Virgil. *American Painting: History and Interpretation.* New York, 1950.

14 BLACK, Mary, and Jean LIPMAN. *American Folk Painting.* New York, 1966.

15 BLOCH, E. Maurice. *George Caleb Bingham: The Evolution of an Artist.* Berkeley, 1967.

16 CRAVEN, Wayne. *Sculpture in America.* New York, 1968.

17 FLEXNER, James Thomas. *That Wilder Image: The Painting of America's Native School from Thomas Cole to Winslow Homer.* Boston, 1962.

18 MC DERMOTT, John Francis. *George Caleb Bingham, River Portraitist.* Norman, Okla., 1959.

19 MILLER, Dorothy. *The Life and Work of David G. Blythe.* Pittsburgh, 1950.

20 MILLER, Lillian B. "Painting, Sculpture, and the National Character, 1815–1860." *J Am Hist*, LIV(1967):696–707.

1 TAFT, Lorado. *The History of American Sculpture*. New York, 1903.

2 THORP, Margaret. *The Literary Sculptors*. Durham, N.C., 1965.

D. Music

3 HATCH, Christopher. "Music for America: A Critical Controversy of the 1850's." *Am Q*, XIV(1962):578–586.

4 HOWARD, John Tasker. *Our American Music: A Comprehensive History from 1620 to the Present*. 4th ed. New York, 1965. (First published in 1931.)

5 HOWARD, John Tasker. *Stephen Foster, America's Troubadour*. New York, 1934.

6 SHULTZ, Gladys Denny. *Jenny Lind, the Swedish Nightingale*. Philadelphia, 1962. (Emphasizes her American tour.)

7 WALTERS, Raymond. *Stephen Foster . . . His Life and Background in Cincinnati, 1846–1850*. Princeton, 1936.

8. Journalism

A. General

8 MOTT, Frank Luther. *American Journalism, 1690–1960*. 3rd ed. New York 1962.

9 MOTT, Frank Luther. *A History of American Magazines*. 5 vols. Cambridge, Mass., 1930–1968. (Particularly, Vols. I and II.)

10 WEISBERGER, Bernard A. *The American Newspaperman*. Chicago, 1961.

11 WOOD, James P. *Magazines in the United States*. 2nd ed., New York 1956.

B. Special Studies

12 ANDERSEN, Arlow William. *The Immigrant Takes His Stand: The Norwegian-American Press and Public Affairs, 1847–1872*. Northfield, Minn., 1953.

13 CHAMBERLIN, Joseph Edgar. *The Boston Transcript: A History of Its First Hundred Years*. Boston, 1930.

14 DABNEY, Thomas Ewing. *One Hundred Great Years: The Story of the Times-Picayune from Its Founding to 1940*. Baton Rouge, 1944.

15 DEMAREE, Albert L. *The American Agricultural Press*. See 42.1.

16 NEVINS, Allan. *The Evening Post: A Century of Journalism*. New York, 1922.

17 NOEL, Mary. *Villains Galore: The Heyday of the Popular Story Weekly*. New York, 1954.

18 SMITH, J. Eugene. *One Hundred Years of Hartford's Courant, from Colonial Times through the Civil War*. New Haven, Conn., 1949.

1 WEISBERGER, Bernard A. *Reporters for the Union.* Boston, 1953.

2 WITTKE, Carl F. *The German-Language Press in America.* Lexington, Ky., 1957.

C. *Biography*
(Listed alphabetically by subject)

3 CARLSON, Oliver. *The Man Who Made News: James Gordon Bennett.* New York, 1942.

4 SEITZ, Don C. *The James Gordon Bennetts, Father and Son.* Indianapolis, 1928.

5 CLAPP, Margaret. *Forgotten First Citizen: John Bigelow.* Boston, 1947. (Editor of New York *Evening Post* in 1850's.)

6 MERRIAM, George S. *The Life and Times of Samuel Bowles.* 2 vols. New York, 1885. (Springfield, Mass., *Republican.*)

7 GODWIN, Parke. *A Biography of William Cullen Bryant.* 2 vols. New York, 1883.

8 MILNE, Gordon. *George William Curtis and the Genteel Tradition.* Bloomington, Ind., 1956.

9 WILSON, James Harrison. *The Life of Charles A. Dana.* New York, 1907. (New York *Tribune.*)

10 SKIPPER, Ottis Clark. *J. D. B. DeBow, Magazinist of the Old South.* Athens, Ga., 1958.

11 GREELEY, Horace. *Recollections of a Busy Life.* New York, 1868.

12 VAN DEUSEN, Glyndon G. *Horace Greeley, Nineteenth Century Crusader.* Philadelphia, 1953.†

13 BROWN, Francis. *Raymond of the Times.* New York, 1951.

14 *Memoirs of Henry Villard, Journalist and Financier, 1835–1900.* 2 vols. New York, 1904.

9. *Theater*

15 BARNES, Eric Wollencott. *The Lady of Fashion: The Life and the Theatre of Anna Cora Mowatt.* New York, 1954.

16 DORMON, James H., Jr. *Theater in the Ante-Bellum South, 1815–1861.* Chapel Hill, N.C., 1967.

17 DOWNER, Alan S. *The Eminent Tragedian, William Charles Macready* Cambridge, Mass., 1966. (Particularly, Chapter VII, for Macready's rivalry with Edwin Forrest.)

18 GRIMSTEAD, David. *Melodrama Unveiled: American Theater and Culture, 1800–1850.* Chicago, 1968.

19 HODGE, Francis. *Yankee Theater: The Image of America on the Stage.* Austin, 1964.

20 HOOLE, W. Stanley. *The Ante-Bellum Charleston Theatre.* Tuscaloosa, Ala., 1946.

21 KENDALL, John S. *The Golden Age of the New Orleans Theater.* Baton Rouge, 1952.

1   MAC MINN, George R. *The Theater of the Golden Era in California.* Caldwell, Idaho, 1941.

2   MOODY, Richard. *America Takes the Stage: Romanticism in American Drama and Theatre, 1750–1900.* Bloomington, Ind., 1955.

3   MOODY, Richard. *Edwin Forrest, First Star of the American Stage.* New York, 1960.

4   MOSES, Montrose J. *The Fabulous Forrest.* Boston, 1929.

5   ODELL, George C. D. *Annals of the New York Stage.* 15 vols. New York, 1927–1949. (Particularly, Vols. IV–VII.)

6   QUINN, Arthur H. *A History of the American Drama, from the Beginning to the Civil War.* New York, 1923.

7   ROURKE, Constance Mayfield. *Troupers of the Gold Coast; or the Rise of Lotta Crabtree.* New York, 1928.

8   RUGGLES, Eleanor. *Prince of Players: Edwin Booth.* New York, 1953.

10. Minor Arts and Popular Culture

9   CHRISTENSEN, Erwin O. *The Index of American Design.* New York, 1950. (Crafts and folk arts.)

10   COMSTOCK, Helen. *American Furniture: Seventeenth, Eighteenth, and Nineteenth Century Styles.* New York, 1962.

11   DAVENPORT, F. Garvin. *Cultural Life in Nashville on the Eve of the Civil War.* Chapel Hill, N.C., 1941.

12   EHRLICH, George. "Technology and the Artist: A Study of the Interaction of Technological Growth and 19th Century American Pictorial Art." Doctoral dissertation, University of Illinois, 1960.

13   GLOAG, John. *Victorian Comfort: A Social History of Design from 1830–1900.* New York, 1961. (Primarily about England, but with many sidelights on the United States.)

14   GRAHAM, Philip. *Showboats: The History of an American Institution.* Austin, 1951.

15   GREEN, Fletcher M. "Listen to the Eagle Scream: One Hundred Years of the Fourth of July in North Carolina." *N C Hist Rev,* XXXI(1954):295–320, 529–549.

16   HIRSCHFIELD, Charles. "America on Exhibition: The New York Crystal Palace." *Am Q,* IX(1957):101–116. (First American world's fair, 1853.)

17   LOMAX, Alan. *The Folk Songs of North America in the English Language.* Garden City, N.Y., 1960.

18   MC DERMOTT, John Francis. *The Lost Panoramas of the Mississippi.* Chicago, 1958.

19   MINNIGERODE, Meade. *The Fabulous Forties, 1840–1850.* Garden City, N.Y., 1924.

20   NATHAN, Hans. *Dan Emmett and the Rise of Early Negro Minstrelsy.* Norman, Okla., 1962.

1 RUDISILL, Richard C. "Mirror Image: The Influence of the Daguerreotype on American Society." Doctoral dissertation, University of Minnesota, 1967.

2 STONE, James H. "The Merchant and the Muse: Commercial Influences on American Popular Music before the Civil War." *Bus Hist Rev*, XXX(1956):1–17.

3 WERNER, M. R. *Barnum*. New York, 1923.

4 WITTKE, Carl F. *Tambo and Bones: A History of the American Minstrel Stage*. Durham, N. C., 1930.

VII. Slavery and the Sectional Conflict

1. Bibliography, Historiography, and Causal Explanation

A. General

5 POTTER, David M. *The South and the Sectional Conflict*. Baton Rouge, 1968. (Particularly, Chapter IV: "The Literature on the Background of the Civil War," extensive revision of an essay in William H. Cartwright and Richard L. Watson, Jr., eds., *Interpreting and Teaching American History*, 31st Yearbook, National Council for the Social Studies, Washington, 1961.)

6 RANDALL, J. G., and David DONALD. *The Civil War and Reconstruction*. 2nd ed. Boston, 1961. (Contains an 86-page critical bibliography, about half of which is relevant to the antebellum period.)

B. The South, Slavery, and Antislavery

7 ALEXANDER, Thomas B. "Historical Treatments of the Dred Scott Case." See 25.15.

8 ALLIS, Frederick S., Jr. "The Dred Scott Labyrinth." See 25.16.

9 DILLON, Merton L. "The Abolitionists: A Decade of Historiography, 1959–1969." *J S Hist*, XXXV(1969):500–522.

10 DUMOND, Dwight Lowell. *A Bibliography of Antislavery in America*. Ann Arbor, Mich., 1961. (Contemporary materials only.)

11 FILLER, Louis. *The Crusade Against Slavery, 1830–1860*. New York, 1960.† (Bibliography, pp. 281–303.)

12 GENOVESE, Eugene D. "Marxian Interpretations of the Slave South." *Towards a New Past: Dissenting Essays in American History*. Ed. by Barton J. Bernstein. New York, 1968.

13 GENOVESE, Eugene D. "Race and Class in Southern History: An Appraisal of the Work of Ulrich Bonnell Phillips." *Ag Hist*, XLI(1967):345–358. (Comments by David M. Potter, Kenneth M. Stampp, and Stanley M. Elkins, pp. 359–371.)

14 LINDEN, Fabian. "Economic Democracy in the Slave South: An Appraisal of Some Recent Views." *J Neg Hist*, XXXI(1946):140–189.

15 LINK, Arthur S., and Rembert W. PATRICK, eds. *Writing Southern History: Essays in Historiography in Honor of Fletcher M. Green*. Baton Rouge, 1965.†

16 STAMPP, Kenneth M. "The Historian and Southern Negro Slavery." *Am Hist Rev*, LVII(1952):613–624. (On U. B. Phillips.)

17 WOODMAN, Harold D. "The Profitability of Slavery." See 38.8.

C. The Coming of the Civil War

1 BEALE, Howard K. "What Historians Have Said about the Causes of the Civil War." *Theory and Practice in Historical Study*. Bulletin 54, Social Science Research Council. New York, 1946. (The pioneer work in modern Civil War historiography.)

2 BENSON, Lee, and Cushing STROUT. "Causation and the American Civil War: Two Appraisals." *Hist Theory*, I(1961):163–185.

3 BONNER, Thomas N. "Civil War Historians and the 'Needless War' Doctrine." *J Hist Ideas*, XVII(1956):193–216.

4 CAMPBELL, A. E. "An Excess of Isolation: Isolation and the American Civil War." *J S Hist*, XXIX(1963):161–174.

5 CRAVEN, Avery. *An Historian and the Civil War*. Chicago, 1964.† (Collection of essays.)

6 DONALD, David. "American Historians and the Causes of the Civil War." *S Atl Q*, LIX(1960):351–355.

7 DRAY, William. "Some Causal Accounts of the American Civil War." *Daedalus*, XCI(1962):578–592. (Comment by Newton Garver, pp. 592–598.)

8 DURKIN, Joseph T. "The Thought That Caused a War: The Compact Theory in the North." *Md Hist Mag*, LVI(1961):1–14.

9 FEHRENBACHER, Don E. *The Changing Image of Lincoln in American Historiography*. Oxford, England, 1968. (Pamphlet.)

10 FEHRENBACHER, Don E. "Disunion and Reunion." *The Reconstruction of American History*. See 9.7.

11 GEYL, Pieter. "The American Civil War and the Problem of Inevitability." *N Eng Q*, XXIV(1951):147–168. (Repr. in 81.2.)

12 JEFFREY, Kirk, Jr. "Stephen Arnold Douglas in American Historical Writing." *J Ill St Hist Soc*, LXI(1968):248–268.

13 JOHANNSEN, Robert W. "In Search of the Real Lincoln, or Lincoln at the Crossroads." *J Ill St Hist Soc*, LXI(1968):229–247.

14 MOORE, Barrington, Jr. *Social Origins of Dictatorship and Democracy*. Boston, 1966.† (Chapter III is on the American Civil War.)

15 NICHOLS, Roy F. "The Kansas-Nebraska Act: A Century of Historiography." *Miss Val Hist Rev*, XLIII(1956):187–212.

16 OWSLEY, Frank L. "The Fundamental Cause of the Civil War: Egocentric Sectionalism." *J S Hist*, VII(1941):3–18.

17 POTTER, David M. *The Lincoln Theme and American National Historiography*. Oxford, England, 1948. (Pamphlet, repr. in *The South and the Sectional Conflict*. See 79.5.)

18 PRESSLY, Thomas J. *Americans Interpret Their Civil War*. Princeton, 1954.† (The most extensive study of Civil War historiography.)

19 RANDALL, J. G. *Lincoln the Liberal Statesman*. New York, 1947.† (Particularly, Chapter II: "A Blundering Generation.")

1 ROSENBERG, John S. "Toward a New Civil War Revisionism." *Am Schol*, XXXVIII(1969):250–272.

2 ROZWENC, Edwin C., ed. *The Causes of the American Civil War*. Boston, 1961.† (Anthology in "Problems in American Civilization" series.)

3 SCHLESINGER, Arthur M., Jr. "The Causes of the American Civil War: A Note on Historical Sentimentalism." *Partisan Rev*, XVI(1949):969–981. (Reprinted in 81.2.)

4 STAMPP, Kenneth M., ed. *The Causes of the Civil War*. Englewood Cliffs, N.J., 1959.†

5 WOOSTER, Ralph A. "The Secession of the Lower South: An Examination of Changing Interpretations." *Civ War Hist*, VII(1961):117–127.

2. Selected Source Materials

6 ANGLE, Paul M., ed. *Created Equal? The Complete Lincoln-Douglas Debates of 1858*. Chicago, 1958. (Contains additional material, especially newspaper reports. There is also a paperback edition of the debates edited by Robert W. Johannsen, New York, 1965.)

7 BREWERTON, G. Douglas. *The War in Kansas*. New York, 1856. (New York *Herald* correspondent.)

8 CATTERALL, Helen Tunnicliff, ed. *Judicial Cases Concerning American Slavery and the Negro*. *Car Inst Pub*, No. 374. 5 vols. Washington, 1926–1937.

9 CHASE, Salmon P. *Diary and Correspondence*. *Ann Rep Am Hist Assn, 1902*, II.

10 DUMOND, Dwight Lowell, ed. *Southern Editorials on Secession*. New York, 1931.

11 HELPER, Hinton Rowan. *The Impending Crisis of the South*. New York, 1857.

12 JAFFA, Harry V., and Robert W. JOHANNSEN. *In the Name of the People: Speeches and Writings of Lincoln and Douglas in the Ohio Campaign of 1859*. Columbus, Ohio, 1959.

13 JONES, Katharine M., ed. *The Plantation South*. Indianapolis, 1957. (Selections from visitors' accounts.)

14 MC KITRICK, Eric L., ed. *Slavery Defended: The Views of the Old South*. Englewood Cliffs, N.J., 1963.†

15 NELSON, Truman, ed. *Documents of Upheaval: Selections from William Lloyd Garrison's "The Liberator," 1831–1865*. New York, 1966.

16 PEASE, William H., and Jane H. PEASE, eds. *The Antislavery Argument*. Indianapolis, 1965.

17 PERKINS, Howard C., ed. *Northern Editorials on Seccession*. 2 vols. New York, 1942.

18 PHILLIPS, Ulrich Bonnell, ed. *The Correspondence of Robert Toombs, Alexander H. Stephens, and Howell Cobb*. *Ann Rep Am Hist Assn, 1911*, II.

1 THOMAS, John L., ed. *Slavery Attacked: The Abolitionist Crusade.* Englewood Cliffs, N.J., 1965.†

2 WISH, Harvey, ed. *Slavery in the South: First-Hand Accounts.* New York, 1964.†

3. *General Studies*

3 BARKER, Alan. *The Civil War in America.* Garden City, N.Y., 1961.†

4 BESTOR, Arthur. "The American Civil War as a Constitutional Crisis." See 26.17.

5 BESTOR, Arthur. "State Sovereignty and Slavery: A Reinterpretation of Proslavery Constitutional Doctrine, 1846–1860." *J Ill St Hist Soc*, LIV(1961): 117–180.

6 BOUCHER, Chauncey S. *"In Re* That Aggressive Slavocracy." *Miss Val Hist Rev*, VIII(1921):13–79.

7 COLE, Arthur Charles. *The Irrepressible Conflict.* See 53.6.

8 CRAVEN, Avery. *Civil War in the Making, 1815–1860.* Baton Rouge, 1959.†

9 CRAVEN, Avery. *The Coming of the Civil War.* New York, 1942.†

10 CRAVEN, Avery. *The Repressible Conflict.* Baton Rouge, 1939.

11 DAVIS, Jefferson. *The Rise and Fall of the Confederate Government.* 2 vols. New York, 1881.

12 DUMOND, Dwight Lowell. *Antislavery Origins of the Civil War in the United States.* Ann Arbor, Mich., 1939.†

13 FONER, Philip S. *Business and Slavery: The New York Merchants and the Irrepressible Conflict.* Chapel Hill, N.C., 1941.

14 JOHNSON, Gerald W. *Secession of the Southern States.* New York, 1933.

15 LLOYD, Arthur Y. *The Slavery Controversy, 1831–1860.* Chapel Hill, N.C., 1939.

16 MACY, Jesse. *The Anti-Slavery Crusade.* New Haven, Conn., 1919.

17 NICHOLS, Roy F. *Blueprints for Leviathan: American Style.* New York, 1963.

18 PHILLIPS, Ulrich Bonnell. *The Course of the South to Secession.* New York, 1939.†

19 QUAIFE, Milo Milton. *The Doctrine of Non-Intervention with Slavery in the Territories.* Chicago, 1910.

20 RANDALL, J. G., and David DONALD. *The Civil War and Reconstruction.* See 79.6.

21 RUSSEL, Robert R. "Constitutional Doctrines with Regard to Slavery in the Territories." *J S Hist*, XXXII(1966):466–486.

22 SIMMS, Henry H. *A Decade of Sectional Controversy, 1851–1861.* Chapel Hill, N.C., 1942.

1 SMITH, Theodore Clarke. *Parties and Slavery, 1850–1859.* New York, 1906.

2 STEPHENS, Alexander H. *A Constitutional View of the Late War between the States.* 2 vols. Philadelphia, 1868–1870.

3 WHITRIDGE, Arnold. *No Compromise! The Story of the Fanatics Who Paved the Way to the Civil War.* New York, 1960.

4 WILSON, Henry. *History of the Rise and Fall of the Slave Power in America.* 3 vols. Boston, 1872–1877.

4. The South

A. General

5 CARPENTER, Jesse T. *The South as a Conscious Minority, 1789–1861.* New York, 1930.

6 CASH, W. J. *The Mind of the South.* New York, 1941.† (Seminal work.)

7 CRAVEN, Avery. *The Growth of Southern Nationalism, 1848–1861.* Baton Rouge, 1953.

8 DODD, William E. *The Cotton Kingdom.* New Haven, Conn., 1919.

9 EATON, Clement. *The Growth of Southern Civilization, 1790–1860.* New York, 1961.†

10 EATON, Clement. *A History of the Old South.* 2nd ed. New York, 1966.

11 FLOAN, Howard R. *The South in Northern Eyes, 1831–1861.* Austin, 1958.

12 GOVAN, Thomas P. "Americans below the Potomac." *The Southerner as American.* Ed. by Charles G. Sellers. Chapel Hill, N.C., 1960.†

13 HARTZ, Louis. *The Liberal Tradition in America.* New York, 1955.† (Particularly, Part Four: "The Feudal Dream of the South.")

14 HUNDLEY, D. R. *Social Relations in Our Southern States.* New York, 1860.

15 PHILLIPS, Ulrich Bonnell. *Life and Labor in the Old South.* Boston, 1929.†

16 PHILLIPS, Ulrich Bonnell. *The Slave Economy of the Old South: Selected Essays in Economic and Social History.* Ed. by Eugene D. Genovese. Baton Rouge, 1968.†

17 POTTER, David M. *The South and the Sectional Conflict.* See 79.5.

18 SAVAGE, Henry, Jr. *Seeds of Time: The Background of Southern Thinking.* New York, 1959.

19 SHRYOCK, Richard Harrison. "Cultural Factors in the History of the South." *J S Hist,* V(1939):333–346.

20 STEPHENSON, Wendell Holmes. *A Basic History of the Old South.* Princeton, 1959.† (Anvil Book, brief and partly documentary.)

1 SYDNOR, Charles S. *The Development of Southern Sectionalism, 1819–1848.* Baton Rouge, 1948.†

2 SYDNOR, Charles S. "The Southerner and the Laws." *J S Hist*, VI(1940):3–23.

B. *Special Studies*

3 COLLINS, Herbert. "The Southern Industrial Gospel before 1860." *J S Hist*, XII(1946):386–402.

4 EATON, Clement. *Freedom of Thought in the Old South.* Durham, N.C., 1940.† (Paperback title varies slightly.)

5 EATON, Clement. *The Mind of the Old South.* See 68.9.

6 EATON, Clement. "Mob Violence in the Old South." *Miss Val Hist Rev*, XXIX(1942):351–370.

7 FRANKLIN, John Hope. *The Militant South, 1800–1861.* Cambridge, Mass., 1956.†

8 GAINES, Francis Pendleton. *The Southern Plantation: A Study in the Development and the Accuracy of a Tradition.* New York, 1925.

9 GREEN, Fletcher M. "Democracy in the Old South." *J S Hist*, XII(1946):3–23.

10 HILLDRUP, Robert LeRoy. "Cold War against the Yankees in the Ante-Bellum Literature of Southern Women." *N C Hist Rev*, XXXI(1954):370–384.

11 JORDAN, Weymouth T. *Rebels in the Making: Planters' Conventions and Southern Propaganda.* Tuscaloosa, Ala., 1958.

12 MENN, Joseph Karl. *The Large Slaveholders of the Deep South, 1860.* New Orleans, 1964. (Statistical.)

13 OSTERWEIS, Rollin G. *Romanticism and Nationalism in the Old South.* New Haven, Conn., 1949.†

14 OWSLEY, Frank L. *Plain Folk of the Old South.* Baton Rouge, 1949.†

15 OWSLEY, Frank L. and Harriet. "The Economic Basis of Society in the Late Antebellum South." *J S Hist*, VI(1940):24–45.

16 ROTHSTEIN, Morton. "The Antebellum South as a Dual Economy: A Tentative Hypothesis." *Ag Hist*, XLI(1967):373–382.

17 RUSSEL, Robert R. *Economic Aspects of Southern Sectionalism, 1840–1861.* Urbana, Ill., 1924.

18 SCARBOROUGH, William K. *The Overseer: Plantation Management in the Old South.* Baton Rouge, 1966.

19 TAYLOR, William R. *Cavalier and Yankee: The Old South and American National Character.* New York, 1961.†

20 THOMPSON, Edgar T. "The Climatic Theory of the Plantation." *Ag Hist*, XV(1941):49–60. (Sociological.)

5. *Slavery*

A. General

1 BOTKIN, B. A., ed. *Lay My Burden Down: A Folk History of Slavery.* Chicago, 1945. (Recorded oral reminiscences.)

2 ELKINS, Stanley M. *Slavery, a Problem in American Institutional and Intellectual Life.* 2nd ed. Chicago, 1968.†

3 FRANKLIN, John Hope. *From Slavery to Freedom.* See 56.17.

4 GENOVESE, Eugene D. *The Political Economy of Slavery.* New York, 1965.†

5 HOLLANDER, Barnett. *Slavery in America: Its Legal History.* London, 1962.

6 JENKINS, William S. *Pro-Slavery Thought in the Old South.* Chapel Hill, N.C., 1935.

7 PHILLIPS, Ulrich Bonnell. *American Negro Slavery.* New York, 1918.†

8 SELLERS, Charles G. "The Travail of Slavery." *The Southerner as American.* See 83.12.

9 STAMPP, Kenneth M. *The Peculiar Institution: Slavery in the Ante-Bellum South.* New York, 1956.†

10 WADE, Richard C. *Slavery in the Cities: The South, 1820–1860.* New York, 1964.†

11 WEINSTEIN, Allen, and Frank Otto GATELL, eds. *American Negro Slavery: A Modern Reader.* New York, 1968.†

12 WOODMAN, Harold D., ed. *Slavery and the Southern Economy.* New York, 1966.†

B. The Slave Trade

13 BANCROFT, Frederic. *Slave-Trading in the Old South.* Baltimore, 1931.

14 BERNSTEIN, Barton J. "Southern Politics and Attempts to Reopen the African Slave Trade." *J Neg Hist*, LI(1966):16–35.

15 DUIGAN, Peter, and Clarence CLENDENEN. *The United States and the African Slave Trade, 1619–1862.* Stanford, 1963.

16 DUBOIS, W. E. Burghardt. *The Suppression of the African Slave Trade to the United States of America, 1638–1870.* New York, 1896.

17 HOWARD, Warren S. *American Slavers and the Federal Law, 1837–1862,* Berkeley, 1963.

18 LANDRY, Harral E. "Slavery and the Slave Trade . . . ." See 30.9.

19 MANNIX, Daniel P., and Malcolm COWLEY. *Black Cargoes: A History of the Atlantic Slave Trade, 1518–1865.* New York, 1962.

1 WISH, Harvey. "The Revival of the African Slave Trade in the United States, 1856–1860." *Miss Val Hist Rev*, XXVII(1941):569–588.

C. State and Local Studies
(Listed geographically by states.)

2 BASSETT, John Spencer. *Slavery in the State of North Carolina. Stud Hist Pol Sci* (Hop), XVII. Baltimore, 1899.

3 PHIFER, Edward W. "Slavery in Microcosm: Burke County, North Carolina." *J S Hist*, XXVIII(1962):137–165.

4 TAYLOR, Rosser H. *Slaveholding in North Carolina: An Economic View.* Chapel Hill, N.C., 1926.

5 HENRY, H. M. *The Police Control of the Slave in South Carolina.* Emory, Va., 1914.

6 FLANDERS, Ralph Betts. *Plantation Slavery in Georgia.* Chapel Hill, N.C., 1933.

7 SELLERS, James B. *Slavery in Alabama.* University, Ala., 1950.

8 SYDNOR, Charles S. *Slavery in Mississippi.* New York, 1933.†

9 TAYLOR, Joe Gray. *Negro Slavery in Louisiana.* Baton Rouge, 1963.

10 REINDERS, Robert C. "Slavery in New Orleans in the Decade before the Civil War." *Mid-Am*, XLIV(1962):211–221.

11 MOONEY, Chase C. *Slavery in Tennessee.* Bloomington, Ind., 1957.

12 COLEMAN, J. Winston, Jr. *Slavery Times in Kentucky.* Chapel Hill, N.C., 1940.

13 TAYLOR, Orville W. *Negro Slavery in Arkansas.* Durham, N.C., 1958.

14 TREXLER, Harrison A. *Slavery in Missouri, 1804–1865. Stud Hist Pol Sci*(Hop):XXXII. Baltimore, 1914.

15 ADDINGTON, Wendell G. "Slave Insurrections in Texas." *J Neg Hist*, XXXV(1950):408–434.

D. Other Special Studies
(For churches and slavery, see 63.11–64.5.)

16 APTHEKER, Herbert. *American Negro Slave Revolts.* New York, 1943.

17 BAUER, Raymond A. and Alice H. BAUER "Day to Day Resistance to Slavery." *J Neg Hist*, XXVII(1942):388–419.

18 BURKE, Joseph C. "What Did the Prigg Decision Really Decide?" See 27.1.

19 CAMPBELL, Stanley Wallace. "Enforcement of the Fugitive Slave Law, 1850–1860." Doctoral dissertation, University of North Carolina, 1967.

20 CARROLL, Joseph Cephas. *Slave Insurrections in the United States, 1800–1865.* Boston, 1938.

1 CONRAD, Alfred H., and John R. MEYER. *The Economics of Slavery, and Other Studies in Econometric History.* Chicago, 1964.

2 EATON, Clement. "Slave Hiring in the Upper South: A Step toward Freedom." *Miss Val Hist Rev*, XLVI(1960):663–678.

3 FREDERICKSON, George M., and Christopher LASCH. "Resistance to Slavery." *Civ War Hist*, XIII(1967):315–329.

4 GARA, Larry. "The Fugitive Slave Law: A Double Paradox." *Civ War Hist*, X(1964):229–240.

5 GOVAN, Thomas P. "Was Plantation Slavery Profitable?" *J S Hist*, VIII(1942):513–535.

6 GRAY, Lewis Cecil. "Economic Efficiency and Competitive Advantages of Slavery under the Plantation System." *Ag Hist*, IV(1930):31–47.

7 GUILLORY, James Denny. "The Pro-Slavery Arguments of Dr. Samuel A· Cartwright." *La Hist*, IX(1968):209–227.

8 MILLER, William L. "Slavery and the Population of the South." *S Econ J*, XXVIII(1961):46–54.

9 MORROW, Ralph E. "The Proslavery Argument Revisited." *Miss Val Hist Rev*, XLVIII(1961):79–94.

10 PERKINS, Howard C. "The Defense of Slavery in the Northern Press on the Eve of the Civil War." *J S Hist*, IX(1943):501–531.

11 RAMSDELL, Charles W. "The Natural Limits of Slavery Expansion." *Miss Val Hist Rev*, XVI(1929):151–171.

12 RUSSEL, Robert R. "The General Effects of Slavery upon Southern Economic Progress." *J S Hist*, IV(1938):34–54.

13 SARAYDAR, Edward. "A Note on the Profitability of Ante-Bellum Slavery." *S Econ J*, XXX(1964):325–332.

14 "Slavery as an Obstacle to Economic Growth in the United States: A Panel Discussion." *J Econ Hist*, XXVII(1967):518–560.

15 SUTCH, Richard. "The Profitability of Antebellum Slavery Revisited." *S Econ J.* XXXI(1965):365–377. (Reply by Edward Saraydar, pp. 377–383.)

16 TANDY, Jeannette Reed. "Pro-Slavery Propaganda in American Fiction of the Fifties." *S Atl Q*, XXI(1922):41–50, 170–178.

17 WISH, Harvey. "The Slave Insurrection Panic of 1856." *J S Hist*, V(1939):206–222.

18 WOOLFOLK, George R. "Planter Capitalism and Slavery: The Labor Thesis." *J Neg Hist*, XLI(1956):103–116.

6. *The Antislavery Movement*

A. *General*

19 BARNES, Gilbert Hobbes. *The Antislavery Impulse, 1830–1844.* New York, 1933.†

1 CURRY, Richard O., ed. *The Abolitionists: Reformers or Fanatics?* New York, 1965.† (Anthology in "American Problems Studies" series.)

2 DILLON, Merton L. "The Failure of American Abolitionists." *J S Hist*, XXV(1959):159–177.

3 DONALD, David. "Toward a Reconsideration of the Abolitionists," in his *Lincoln Reconsidered.* 2nd ed., enlarged. New York, 1961.†

4 DUBERMAN, Martin B., ed. *The Antislavery Vanguard: New Essays on the Abolitionists.* Princeton, 1965.†

5 DUMOND, Dwight Lowell. *Antislavery: The Crusade for Freedom in America.* Ann Arbor, Mich., 1961.†

6 FILLER, Louis. *The Crusade against Slavery.* See 79.11.

7 FLADELAND, Betty. "Who Were the Abolitionists?" *J Neg Hist*, XLIX(1964):99–115.

8 KRADITOR, Aileen S. *Means and Ends in American Abolitionism.* New York, 1969.

9 LADER, Lawrence. *The Bold Brahmins: New England's War against Slavery, 1831–1863.* New York, 1961.

10 LUTZ, Alma. *Crusade for Freedom: Women of the Antislavery Movement.* Boston, 1968.

11 MATHEWS, Donald G. "The Abolitionists on Slavery: The Critique behind the Social Movement." *J S Hist*, XXXIII(1967):163–182.

12 NYE, Russel B. *Fettered Freedom: Civil Liberties and the Slavery Controversy, 1830–1860.* East Lansing, Mich., 1949.

13 PERRY, Lewis Curtis. "Antislavery and Anarchy: A Study of the Ideas of Abolitionism before the Civil War." Doctoral dissertation, Cornell University, 1967.

14 QUARLES, Benjamin. *Black Abolitionists.* New York, 1969.

15 RIETVELD, Ronald Deane. "The Moral Issue of Slavery in American Politics, 1854–1860." Doctoral dissertation, University of Illinois, 1967.

16 SIMMS, Henry H. *Emotion at High Tide: Abolition as a Controversial Factor, 1830–1845.* Richmond, 1960.

17 SMITH, Theodore Clarke. *The Liberty and Free Soil Parties . . . .* See 32.3.

18 TREFOUSSE, Hans L. *The Radical Republicans.* New York, 1969.

B. *Special Studies*

19 BERWANGER, Eugene H. *The Frontier against Slavery: Western Anti-Negro Prejudice and the Slavery Extension Controversy.* Urbana, Ill., 1967.

20 BUCKMASTER, Henrietta. *Let My People Go: The Story of the Underground Railroad and the Growth of the Abolition Movement.* New York, 1941. (Romantic treatment.)

21 COLE, Charles C., Jr. "Horace Bushnell and the Slavery Question." *N Eng Q*, XXIII(1950):19–30.

1 DEMOS, John. "The Antislavery Movement and the Problem of Violent Means." *N Eng Q*, XXXVII(1964):501–526.

2 DUVALL, Severn. *"Uncle Tom's Cabin."* See 73.1.

3 GARA, Larry. *The Liberty Line: The Legend of the Underground Railroad.* Lexington, Ky., 1961.†

4 GARA, Larry. "Slavery and the Slave Power: A Crucial Distinction." *Civ War Hist*, XV(1969):5–18.

5 GRIFFIN, Clifford S. "The Abolitionists and the Benevolent Societies, 1831–1861." *J Neg Hist*, XLIV(1959):195–216.

6 LOFTON, Williston H. "Abolition and Labor." See 51.11.

7 MC PHERSON, James M. "The Fight against the Gag Rule: Joshua Leavitt and Antislavery Insurgency in the Whig Party, 1839–1842." *J Neg Hist*, XLVIII(1963):177–195.

8 OSTRANDER, Gilman M. "Emerson, Thoreau, and John Brown." *Miss Val Hist Rev*, XXXIX(1953):713–726.

9 PARKER, Russell Dean. " 'Higher Law': Its Development and Application to the American Antislavery Controversy." Doctoral dissertation, University of Tennessee, 1966.

10 PEASE, William H. and Jane H. PEASE. "Antislavery Ambivalence: Immediatism, Expediency, and Race." *Am Q*, XVII(1965):682–695.

11 QUARLES, Benjamin. "Sources of Abolitionist Income." *Miss Val Hist Rev*, XXXII(1945):63–76.

12 RAYBACK, Joseph G. "The American Workingman and the Antislavery Crusade." See 51.13.

13 SIMMS, Henry H. "A Critical Analysis of Abolition Literature." *J S Hist*, VI(1940):368–382.

14 STEWART, James B. "The Aims and Impact of Garrisonian Abolitionism, 1840–1860." *Civ War Hist*, XV(1969):197–209.

15 WESLEY, Charles H. " . . . Negroes in Anti–Slavery Political Parties." See 57.8.

16 WYATT-BROWN, Bertram. "William Lloyd Garrison and Antislavery Unity, a Reappraisal." *Civ War Hist*, XIII(1967):5–24.

7. *The Crisis of 1850*

17 AMES, Herman V. "John C. Calhoun and the Secession Movement of 1850." *Proc Am Ant Soc*, n.s. XXVIII(1918):19–50.

18 BOUCHER, Chauncey S. *The Secession and Cooperation Movements in South Carolina, 1848–1852. Stud* (Wash), 4th ser. Vol. V. Concord, N.H., 1918.

19 BROOKS, Robert P. "Howell Cobb and the Crisis of 1850." *Miss Val Hist Rev*, IV(1917):279–298.

20 CARMAN, Harry J., and Reinhold H. LUTHIN. "The Seward-Fillmore Feud and the Crisis of 1850." *N Y Hist*, XXIV(1943):163–184.

21 FONER, Eric. "The Wilmot Proviso Revisited." *J Am Hist*, LVI(1969):262–279.

1 FOSTER, Herbert Darling. "Webster's Seventh of March Speech and the Secession Movement, 1850." *Am Hist Rev*, XXVII(1922):245–270.

2 FULLER, John D. P. "Slavery Propaganda During the Mexican War." *SW Hist Q*, XXXVIII(1935):235–245.

3 HAMILTON, Holman. *Prologue to Conflict: The Crisis and Compromise of 1850*. Lexington, Ky., 1964.†

4 HARMON, George D. "Douglas and the Compromise of 1850." *J Ill St Hist Soc*, XXI(1929):453–499.

5 HODDER, Frank Heywood. "The Authorship of the Compromise of 1850." *Miss Val Hist Rev*, XXII(1936):525–536.

6 HUBBELL, John T. "Three Georgia Unionists and the Compromise of 1850." *Ga Hist Q*, LI(1967):307–323.

7 LYNCH, William O. "Zachary Taylor as President." *J S Hist*, IV(1938):279–294.

8 MORRISON, Chaplain W. *Democratic Politics and Sectionalism: The Wilmot Proviso Controversy*. Chapel Hill, N.C., 1967.

9 NORTON, L. Wesley. "The Religious Press and the Compromise of 1850." Doctoral dissertation, University of Illinois, 1959.

10 ROSENBERG, Morton M. "Iowa Politics and the Compromise of 1850." *Iowa J Hist*, LVI(1958):193–206.

11 ROZWENC, Edwin C., ed. *The Compromise of 1850*. Boston, 1957.† (Anthology in "Problems in American Civilization" series.)

12 RUSSEL, Robert R. "What Was the Compromise of 1850?" *J S Hist*, XXII(1956):292–309.

13 SHRYOCK, Richard Harrison. *Georgia and the Union in 1850*. Durham, N.C., 1926.

14 STENBERG, Richard R. "The Motivation of the Wilmot Proviso." *Miss Val Hist Rev*, XVIII(1932):535–541.

15 VAN TASSEL, David D. "Gentlemen of Property and Standing: Compromise Sentiment in Boston in 1850." *N Eng Q*, XXIII(1950):307–319.

16 WHITE, Melvin Johnson. *The Secession Movement in the United States, 1847–1852*. New Orleans, 1916.

17 WILSON, Major L. "Of Time and the Union: Webster and His Critics in the Crisis of 1850." *Civ War Hist*, XIV(1968):293–306.

8. *The Kansas Issue*

18 ANDREWS, Horace, Jr. "Kansas Crusade: Eli Thayer and the New England Emigrant Aid Company." *N Eng Q*, XXXV(1962):497–514.

19 BALTIMORE, Lester B. "Benjamin F. Stringfellow: The Fight for Slavery on the Missouri Border." *Mo Hist Rev*, LXII(1967):14–29.

20 EWY, Marvin. "The United States Army in the Kansas Border Troubles, 1855–1856." *Kan Hist Q*, XXXII(1966):385–400.

1 GAEDDERT, G. Raymond. *The Birth of Kansas.* Lawrence, Kan., 1940.

2 GATES, Paul Wallace. *Fifty Million Acres.* See 16.7.

3 GATES, Paul Wallace. "The Struggle for Land and the 'Irrepressible Conflict.'" See 16.9.

4 HARLOW, Ralph Volney. "The Rise and Fall of the Kansas Aid Movement." *Am Hist Rev,* XLI(1935):1–25.

5 HART, Charles Desmond. "Congressmen and the Expansion of Slavery . . . ." See 28.7.

6 HART, Charles Desmond. "Why Lincoln Said 'No': Congressional Attitudes on Slavery Expansion, 1860–1861." *Soc Sci Q*(1968):732–741.

7 HODDER, Frank Heywood. "The Genesis of the Kansas-Nebraska Act." *Proc St Hist Soc Wis, 1912,* 69–86.

8 HODDER, Frank Heywood. "The Railroad Background of the Kansas-Nebraska Act." *Miss Val Hist Rev,* XII(1925):3–22.

9 JOHANNSEN, Robert W. "The Lecompton Constitutional Convention: An Analysis of Its Membership." *Kan Hist Q,* XXIII(1957):225–243.

10 JOHNSON, Samuel A. *The Battle Cry of Freedom: The New England Emigrant Aid Company in the Kansas Crusade.* Lawrence, Kan., 1954.

11 MALIN, James C. *The Nebraska Question.* See 16.11.

12 MALIN, James C. "The Pro-Slavery Background of the Kansas Struggle." *Miss Val Hist Rev,* X(1923):285–305.

13 MONAGHAN, Jay. *Civil War on the Western Border, 1854–1865.* Boston, 1955.

14 NICHOLS, Alice. *Bleeding Kansas.* New York, 1954.

15 O'CONNOR, Thomas H. "Cotton Whigs in Kansas." *Kan Hist Q,* XXVI(1960):34–58.

16 RAY, P. Orman. *The Repeal of the Missouri Compromise.* Cleveland, 1909.

17 RUSSEL, Robert R. "The Issues in the Congressional Struggle over the Kansas-Nebraska Bill, 1854." *J S Hist,* XXIX(1963):187–210.

18 *Territorial Kansas: Studies Commemorating the Centennial.* Lawrence, Kan., 1954.

9. The Mounting Controversy, 1857–1860

19 AUER, J. Jeffery, ed. *Antislavery and Disunion, 1858–1861: Studies in the Rhetoric of Compromise and Conflict.* New York, 1963.

20 CRENSHAW, Ollinger. "The Speakership Contest of 1859–1860." *Miss Val Hist Rev,* XXIX(1942):323–338.

21 FEHRENBACHER, Don E. *Prelude to Greatness: Lincoln in the 1850's.* Stanford, 1962.†

1 FURNAS, Joseph C. *The Road to Harpers Ferry*. New York, 1959.

2 HECKMAN, Richard A. *Lincoln vs. Douglas: The Great Debates Campaign*. Washington, 1967.

3 HODDER, Frank Heywood. "Some Phases of the Dred Scott Case." *Miss Val Hist Rev*, XVI(1929):3–22.

4 HOPKINS, Vincent C. *Dred Scott's Case*. See 27.9.

5 JAFFA, Harry V. *Crisis of the House Divided: An Interpretation of the Issues in the Lincoln-Douglas Debates*. New York, 1959.

6 JAFFA, Harry V. "Expediency and Morality in the Lincoln-Douglas Debates." *Anchor Review*, No. 2(1957):179–204.

7 JOHANNSEN, Robert W. "Stephen A. Douglas, 'Harper's Magazine,' and Popular Sovereignty." *Miss Val Hist Rev*, XLV(1959):606–631.

8 KELLER, Allan. *Thunder at Harpers Ferry*. Englewood Cliffs, N.J., 1958.†

9 KUTLER, Stanley I., ed. *The Dred Scott Decision*. See 27.11.

10 LUTHIN, Reinhard H. "The Democratic Split during Buchanan's Administration." *Pa Hist*, XI(1944):13–35.

11 MENDELSOHN, Wallace. "Dred Scott's Case Reconsidered." *Minn Law Rev*, XXXVIII(1953):16–28.

12 NICHOLS, Roy F. *The Disruption of American Democracy*. New York, 1948.† (Extensive treatment of the period 1856–1861, unrivaled by any other modern study except Allan Nevins, *The Emergence of Lincoln* [5.12].)

13 WHITRIDGE, Arnold. "The John Brown Legend." *Hist Today*, VII(1957): 211–220.

14 WOODWARD, C. Vann. "John Brown's Private War," in his *The Burden of Southern History*. Baton Rouge, 1960.†

10. Disruption of the Union, 1860–1861

A. General

15 AUCHAMPAUGH, Philip G. *James Buchanan and His Cabinet on the Eve of Secession*. Lancaster, Pa., 1926.

16 BUCHANAN, James. *Mr. Buchanan's Administration on the Eve of the Rebellion*. New York, 1866.

17 CATTON, Bruce. *The Coming Fury*. Garden City, N.Y., 1961.†

18 CHADWICK, French Ensor. *Causes of the Civil War, 1859–1861*. New York, 1906.

19 GARFINKLE, Norton, ed. *Lincoln and the Coming of the Civil War*. Boston, 1959.† (Anthology in "Problems in American Civilization" series.)

20 GLOVER, Gilbert Graffenreid. *Immediate Pre-Civil War Compromise Efforts*. *Contrib Ed* (Peabody), No. 131. Nashville, 1934.

1 GRAEBNER, Norman A., ed. *Politics and the Crisis of 1860.* See 32.7.

2 KNOLES, George H., ed. *The Crisis of the Union, 1860–1861.* Baton Rouge, 1965.

3 NICHOLS, Roy F. *The Disruption of American Democracy.* See 92.12.

4 POTTER, David M. *Lincoln and His Party in the Secession Crisis.* New Haven, Conn., 1942.† (Paperback edition has extensive new preface.)

5 STAMPP, Kenneth M. *And the War Came.* Baton Rouge, 1950.†

B. *The Election of Lincoln*

6 COLE, Arthur Charles. "Lincoln's Election an Immediate Menace to Slavery in the States?" *Am Hist Rev,* XXXVI(1931):740–767. (See the response with the same title by J. G. de Roulhac Hamilton in *ibid.,* XXXVII[1932]:700–711.)

7 CRENSHAW, Ollinger. *The Slave States in the Presidential Election of 1860.* See 32.5.

8 FITE, Emerson David. *The Presidential Campaign of 1860.* See 32.6.

9 LUTHIN, Reinhard H. *The First Lincoln Campaign.* See 32.10.

10 STREVEY, Tracy E. "Joseph Medill and the *Chicago Tribune* in the Nomination and Election of Lincoln." *Pap Ill Hist,* 1938, pp. 39–63.

11 VENABLE, Austin L. "The Conflict between the Douglas and Yancy Forces in the Charleston Convention." *J S Hist,* VIII(1942):226–241.

C. *Secession*

12 ADAMS, Henry. *The Great Secession Winter of 1860–61, and Other Essays.* Ed. by George Hochfield. New York, 1958. (The title essay was originally published in *Proc Mass Hist Soc,* XLIII[1910]:660–687.)

13 BONNER, Thomas N. "Horace Greeley and the Secession Movement, 1860–1861." *Miss Val Hist Rev,* XXXVIII(1951):425–444. (Compare with 94.3.)

14 DUMOND, Dwight Lowell. *The Secession Movement, 1860–1861.* New York, 1931.

15 GUNDERSON, Robert Gray. *Old Gentlemen's Convention: The Washington Peace Conference of 1861.* Madison, Wis., 1961.

16 HECK, Frank H. "John C. Breckinridge in the Crisis of 1860–1861." *J S Hist,* XXI(1955):316–346.

17 HYMAN, Harold M. "The Narrow Escape from a 'Compromise of 1860': Secession and the Constitution." *Freedom and Reform: Essays in Honor of Henry Steele Commager.* Ed. by Harold M. Hyman and Leonard W. Levy. New York, 1967.

1 JOHANNSEN, Robert W. "The Douglas Democracy and the Crisis of Disunion." *Civ War Hist*, IX(1963):229–247.

2 KEENE, Jesse L. *The Peace Convention of 1861*. Tuscaloosa, Ala., 1961.

3 POTTER, David M. "Horace Greeley and Peaceable Secession." *J S Hist*, VII(1941):145–159. (Reprinted in *The South and the Sectional Conflict* [See 93.13.] with a "Postscript" responding to the Bonner article listed above, 93.13.)

4 REYNOLDS, Donald Eugene. "Southern Newspapers in the Secession Crisis, 1860–1861." Doctoral dissertation, Tulane University, 1966.

5 SCRUGHAM, Mary. *The Peaceable Americans of 1860–1861: A Study in Public Opinion*. New York, 1921.

6 SOWLE, Patrick. "The Conciliatory Republicans during the Winter of Secession." Doctoral dissertation, Duke University, 1963.

7 SOWLE, Patrick. "A Reappraisal of Seward's Memorandum of April 1, 1861, to Lincoln." *J S Hist*, XXXIII(1967):234–239.

8 WHITE, Laura A. "Charles Sumner and the Crisis of 1860–1861." *Essays in Honor of William E. Dodd*. Ed. by Avery Craven. Chicago, 1935.

9 WOOSTER, Ralph A. *The Secession Conventions of the South*. Princeton 1962.

D. Fort Sumter

10 CRAWFORD, Samuel W. *The Genesis of the Civil War: The Story of Sumter 1860–1861*. New York, 1887.

11 CURRENT, Richard N. "The Confederates and the First Shot." *Civ War Hist*, VII(1961):357–369.

12 CURRENT, Richard N. *Lincoln and the First Shot*. Philadelphia, 1963.†

13 JOHNSON, Ludwell. "Fort Sumter and Confederate Diplomacy." *J S Hist*, XXVI(1960):441–477.

14 MC WHINEY, Grady. "The Confederacy's First Shot." *Civ War Hist*, XIV(1968):5–14.

15 MEREDITH, Roy. *Storm over Sumter: The Opening Engagement of the Civil War*. New York, 1957.

16 RAMSDELL, Charles W. "Lincoln and Fort Sumter." *J S Hist*, III(1937): 259–288.

17 RANDALL, J. G. "Lincoln's Sumter Dilemma," in his *Lincoln the Liberal Statesman*. See 80.19.

18 SWANBERG, W. A. *First Blood: The Story of Fort Sumter*. New York, 1957.

19 TILLEY, John Shipley. *Lincoln Takes Command*. Chapel Hill, N.C., 1941. (Extremely pro-Southern.)

11. The Sectional Conflict: State and Local Studies
(Listed geographically by states. See also 32.15–35.10.)

1 O'CONNOR, Thomas H. *Cotton Whigs and Union: The Textile Manufacturers of Massachusetts and the Coming of the Civil War.* New York, 1968.

2 LEVY, Leonard W. "Sims' Case: The Fugitive Slave Law in Boston in 1851." *J Neg Hist*, XXXV(1950):39–74.

3 STANLEY, John L. "Majority Tyranny in Tocqueville's America: The Failure of Negro Suffrage in 1846." *Pol Sci Q*, LXXXIV(1969):412–435. (New York.)

4 DUSINBERRE, William. *Civil War Issues in Philadelphia, 1856–1865.* Philadelphia, 1965.

5 AMBLER, Charles H. *Sectionalism in Virginia from 1776 to 1861.* Chicago, 1910.

6 HICKIN, Patricia Elizabeth, "Antislavery in Virginia, 1831–1861." Doctoral dissertation, University of Virginia, 1968.

7 SHANKS, Henry T. *The Secession Movement in Virginia, 1847–1861.* Richmond, 1934.

8 BOYKIN, James H. *North Carolina in 1861.* New York, 1961.

9 SITTERSON, J. Carlyle. *The Secession Movement in North Carolina.* Chapel Hill, N.C., 1939.

10 BOUCHER, Chauncey S. *The Secession and Cooperation Movements in South Carolina.* See 89.18.

11 CAUTHEN, Charles Edward. *South Carolina Goes to War, 1860–1865.* Chapel Hill, N.C., 1950.

12 CHANNING, Steven Alan. "Crisis of Fear: Secession in South Carolina, 1859–1860." Doctoral dissertation, University of North Carolina, 1968.

13 HAMER, Philip M. *The Secession Movement in South Carolina, 1847–1852.* Allentown, Pa., 1918.

14 KIBLER, Lillian A. "Unionist Sentiment in South Carolina in 1860." *J S Hist*, IV(1938):346–366.

15 SCHULTZ, Harold S. *Nationalism and Sectionalism in South Carolina, 1852–1860.* Durham, N.C., 1950.

16 VAN DEUSEN, John G. *Economic Bases of Disunion in South Carolina.* New York, 1928.

17 PHILLIPS, Ulrich Bonnell. *Georgia and State Rights. Ann Rep Am Hist Assn, 1901*, II.†

18 DODD, Dorothy. "The Secession Movement in Florida, 1850–1861." *Fla Hist Q*, XII(1933):3–24, 45–66.

19 THOMPSON, Arthur W. "Political Nativism in Florida, 1848–1860: A Phase of Anti-Secessionism." *J S Hist*, XV(1949):39–65.

20 ALEXANDER, Thomas B., and Peggy J. DUCKWORTH. "Alabama 'Black Belt' Whigs during Secession: A New Viewpoint." *Ala Rev*, XVII(1964):181–197.

1 DENMAN, Clarence P. *The Secession Movement in Alabama.* Montgomery, Ala., 1933.

2 LONG, Durward. "Unanimity and Disloyalty in Secessionist Alabama." *Civ War Hist*, XI(1965):257–273.

3 RAINWATER, Percy L. *Mississippi, Storm Center of Secession, 1856–1861.* Baton Rouge, 1938.

4 CASKEY, Willie Malvin. *Secession and Restoration of Louisiana.* Baton Rouge, 1938.

5 HENDRIX, James Paisley, Jr. "The Efforts to Reopen the African Slave Trade in Louisiana." *La Hist*, X(1969):97–123.

6 SHUGG, Roger W. *Origins of Class Struggle in Louisiana.* Baton Rouge, 1939.

7 CAMPBELL, Mary Emily Robertson. *The Attitude of Tennesseans toward the Union, 1847–1861.* New York, 1961.

8 SIOUSSAT, St. George L. "Tennessee, the Compromise of 1850, and the Nashville Convention." *Miss Val Hist Rev*, II(1915):313–347.

9 SCROGGS, Jack B. "Arkansas in the Secession Crisis." *Ark Hist Q*, XII(1953):179–224.

10 DUNN, Roy Sylvan. "The KGC in Texas, 1860–1861." *SW Hist Q*, LXX(1967):543–573. (Knights of the Golden Circle.)

11 SMYRL, Frank H. "Unionism in Texas, 1856–1861." *SW Hist Q*, LXVIII(1964):172–195.

12 DIKET, A. L. "John Slidell and the 'Chicago Incident' of 1858." *La Hist*, V(1964):369–386.

13 ROSENBERG, Morton M. "The Kansas-Nebraska Act in Iowa: A Case Study." *Ann Iowa*, XXXVII(1964):436–457.

14 ZORN, Roman J. "Minnesota Public Opinion and the Secession Controversy, December, 1860–April, 1861." *Miss Val Hist Rev*, XXXVI(1949):435–456.

15 GANAWAY, Loomis Morton. *New Mexico and the Sectional Controversy, 1846–1861.* Albuquerque, 1944.

16 ELLISON, Joseph. *California and the Nation, 1850–1869. Pub Hist* (Berk), XVI. Berkeley, 1927.

17 JOHANNSEN, Robert W. *Frontier Politics . . . .* See 35.20.

18 JOHANNSEN, Robert W. "The Sectional Crisis and the Frontier: Washington Territory, 1860–1861." *Miss Val Hist Rev*, XXXIX(1952):415–440.

12. Biography

(Listed alphabetically by subject; see also 35.21–38.2.)

A. Adams to Cushing

19 DUBERMAN, Martin B. *Charles Francis Adams, 1807–1886.* Boston, 1961.†

1 PARRISH, William E. *David Rice Atchison of Missouri, Border Politician.* Columbia, Mo., 1961.

2 CAIN, Marvin R. *Lincoln's Attorney General, Edward Bates of Missouri.* Columbia, Mo., 1965.

3 PARKS, Joseph H. *John Bell of Tennessee.* Baton Rouge, 1950.

4 BUTLER, Pierce. *Judah P. Benjamin.* Philadelphia, 1907.

5 MEADE, Robert Douthat. *Judah P. Benjamin, Confederate Statesman.* New York, 1943.

6 RIGGS, C. Russell. "The Ante-Bellum Career of John A. Bingham: A Case Study in the Coming of the Civil War." Doctoral dissertation, New York University, 1959.

7 FLADELAND, Betty. *James Gillespie Birney: Slaveholder to Abolitionist.* Ithaca, N.Y., 1955.

8 BRIGANCE, William N. *Jeremiah Sullivan Black.* Philadelphia, 1934.

9 BOWDITCH, Vincent Y. *Life and Correspondence of Henry Ingersoll Bowditch.* 2 vols. Boston, 1902. (Physician and prominent Abolitionist.)

10 VAN DER WEELE, Wayne J. "Jessie David Bright, Master Politician from the Old Northwest." Doctoral dissertation, Indiana University, 1958.

11 WILLIAMS, David A. *David C. Broderick, a Political Portrait.* San Marino, Calif., 1969.

12 RANCK, James Byrne. *Albert Gallatin Brown, Radical Southern Nationalist.* New York, 1937.

13 MALIN, James C. *John Brown and the Legend of Fifty-Six.* Philadelphia, 1942.

14 RUCHAMES, Louis, ed. *A John Brown Reader.* London, 1959.

15 VILLARD, Oswald Garrison. *John Brown, 1800–1859.* Boston, 1910.

16 BAXTER, Maurice. *Orville H. Browning, Lincoln's Friend and Critic.* Bloomington, Ind., 1957.

17 KLEIN, Philip S. *President James Buchanan: A Biography.* University Park, Pa., 1962.

18 PENDLETON, Lawson Alan. "James Buchanan's Attitude toward Slavery." Doctoral dissertation, University of North Carolina, 1964.

19 BRADLEY, Erwin Stanley. *Simon Cameron, Lincoln's Secretary of War.* Philadelphia, 1966.

20 CRIPPEN, Lee F. *Simon Cameron: Ante-Bellum Years.* Oxford, Ohio, 1942.

21 HARRIS, Wilmer C. *The Public Life of Zachariah Chandler, 1851–1875.* Chicago, 1917.

22 HART, Albert Bushnell. *Salmon Portland Chase.* Cambridge, Mass., 1899.

23 BAER, Helen G. *The Heart Is Like Heaven: The Life of Lydia Maria Child.* Philadelphia, 1964.

1 SMILEY, David L. *Lion of White Hall: The Life of Cassius M. Clay.* Madison, Wis., 1962.

2 CLAY-CLOPTON, Virginia. *A Belle of the Fifties.* Ed. by Ada Sterling. New York, 1904. (Southern woman's view of antebellum Washington.)

3 JOHNSON, Zachary Taylor. *Political Policies of Howell Cobb. Contrib Ed* (Peabody), No. 55. Nashville, 1929.

4 PENDERGRAFT, Daryl. "Thomas Corwin and the Conservative Republican Reaction, 1858–1861." *Ohio Arch Hist Q,* LVII(1948):1–23.

5 LINDSEY, David. *"Sunset Cox": Irrepressible Democrat.* Detroit, 1959

6 KIRWAN, Albert D. *John J. Crittenden: The Struggle for the Union.* Lexington, Ky., 1962.

7 FUESS, Claude M. *The Life of Caleb Cushing.* 2 vols. New York, 1923.

B. Davis to Hunter

8 KING, Willard L. *Lincoln's Manager, David Davis.* Cambridge, Mass., 1960.

9 CATTON, Bruce and William. *Two Roads to Sumter.* New York, 1963. (Jefferson Davis and Abraham Lincoln.)

10 DODD, William E. *Jefferson Davis.* Philadelphia, 1907.

11 MC ELROY, Robert. *Jefferson Davis: The Unreal and the Real,* 2 vols. New York, 1937.

12 STRODE, Hudson. *Jefferson Davis, American Patriot, 1808–1861.* New York, 1955.

13 CAPERS, Gerald M. *Stephen A. Douglas, Defender of the Union.* Boston, 1959.

14 JOHNSON, Allen. *Stephen A. Douglas.* New York, 1908.

15 MILTON, George Fort. *The Eve of Conflict: Stephen A. Douglas and the Needless War.* Boston, 1934.

16 NEVINS, Allan. "Stephen A. Douglas: His Weakness and His Greatness." *J Ill St Hist Soc,* XLII(1949):385–410.

17 STEVENS, Frank E. "Life of Stephen A. Douglas." *J Ill St Hist Soc,* XVI(1924):243–673. (A full-length biography.)

18 QUARLES, Benjamin. *Frederick Douglass.* See 57.4.

19 PELZER, Louis. *Augustus Caesar Dodge.* Iowa City, 1909.

20 JELLISON, Charles A. *Fessenden of Maine, Civil War Senator.* Syracuse, N.Y., 1962.

21 RAYBACK, Robert J. *Millard Fillmore, Biography of a President.* Buffalo, 1959.

22 WISH, Harvey. *George Fitzhugh.* See 71.14.

23 KORNGOLD, Ralph. *Two Friends of Man: The Story of William Lloyd Garrison and Wendell Phillips, and Their Relationship with Abraham Lincoln.* Boston, 1950.

1   MERRILL, Walter M. *Against Wind and Tide: A Biography of Wm. Lloyd Garrison.* Cambridge, Mass., 1963.†

2   NYE, Russel B. *William Lloyd Garrison and the Humanitarian Reformers.* Boston, 1955

3   THOMAS, John L. *The Liberator: William Lloyd Garrison.* Boston, 1963.

4   LUDLUM, Robert. "Joshua Giddings, Radical." *Miss Val Hist Rev,* XXIII(1936):49–60.

5   HALE, William Harlan. *Horace Greeley, Voice of the People.* New York, 1950.

6   ISELY, Jeter A. *Horace Greeley and the Republican Party, 1853–1861.* Princeton, 1947.

7   STODDARD, Henry Luther. *Horace Greeley: Printer, Editor, Crusader.* New York, 1946.

8   VAN DEUSEN, Glyndon G. *Horace Greeley.* See 77.12.

9   SEWELL, Richard H. *John P. Hale and the Politics of Abolition.* Cambridge, Mass., 1965.

10 MERRITT, Elizabeth. *James Henry Hammond, 1807–1864.* Baltimore, 1923.

11 BAILEY, Hugh C. *Hinton Rowan Helper, Abolitionist-Racist.* University, Ala., 1965.

12 CARDOSO, Joaquín José. "Hinton Rowan Helper: A Nineteenth Century Pilgrimage." Doctoral dissertation, University of Wisconsin, 1967.

13 DONALD, David. *Lincoln's Herndon.* New York, 1948.

14 EDELSTEIN, Tilden G. *Strange Enthusiasm: A Life of Thomas Wentworth Higginson.* New Haven, Conn., 1968.

15 SIMMS, Henry H. *Life of Robert M. T. Hunter: A Study in Sectionalism and Secession.* Richmond, 1935.

C. Johnson to Pike

16 FLIPPIN, Percy Scott. *Herschel V. Johnson of Georgia, State Rights Unionist.* Richmond, 1931.

17 JULIAN, George W. *Political Recollections, 1840–1872.* Chicago, 1884.

18 RIDDLEBERGER, Patrick W. *George Washington Julian, Radical Republican.* Indianapolis, 1966.

19 YOUNGER, Edward. *John A. Kasson: Politics and Diplomacy from Lincoln to McKinley.* Iowa City, 1955.

20 MC CORMACK, Thomas J., ed. *Memoirs of Gustave Koerner, 1809–1896.* 2 vols. Cedar Rapids, Iowa, 1909.

21 HENDRICKSON, James E. *Joe Lane of Oregon: Machine Politics and the Sectional Crisis, 1849–1861.* New Haven, Conn., 1967.

22 LAWRENCE, William. *Life of Amos A. Lawrence, with Extracts from His Diary and Correspondence.* Boston, 1888.

1 FREEMAN, Douglas Southall. *R. E. Lee: A Biography*. 4 vols. New York, 1934–1935. (Particularly, Vol. I.)

2 BONEY, F. N. *John Letcher of Virginia*. University, Ala., 1966.

3 BARINGER, William E. *A House Dividing: Lincoln as President Elect*. Springfield, Ill., 1945.

4 BARINGER, William E. *Lincoln's Rise to Power*. Boston, 1937.

5 BEVERIDGE, Albert J. *Abraham Lincoln, 1809–1858*. 2 vols. Boston, 1928.

6 CATTON, Bruce and William. *Two Roads to Sumter*. See 98.9.

7 CURRENT, Richard N. *The Lincoln Nobody Knows*. New York, 1958.†

8 DONALD, David. *Lincoln Reconsidered*. See 88.3.

9 FEHRENBACHER, Don E. *Prelude to Greatness*. See 91.21.

10 GRAEBNER, Norman A., ed. *The Enduring Lincoln*. Urbana, Ill., 1959.

11 HERNDON, William H., and Jesse W. WEIK. *Herndon's Lincoln: The True Story of a Great Life*. 3 vols. Chicago, 1889.†

12 LUTHIN, Reinhard H. *The Real Abraham Lincoln*. Englewood Cliffs, N.J., 1960.

13 RANDALL, J. G. *Lincoln the President: Springfield to Gettysburg*. 2 vols. New York, 1946.

14 SANDBURG, Carl. *Abraham Lincoln: The Prairie Years*. 2 vols. New York, 1926.

15 THOMAS, Benjamin P. *Abraham Lincoln: A Biography*. New York, 1952.

16 MAGDOL, Edward. *Owen Lovejoy, Abolitionist in Congress*. New Brunswick, N.J., 1967.

17 RAWLEY, James A. *Edwin D. Morgan, 1811–1883: Merchant in Politics*. New York, 1955.

18 MITCHELL, Broadus. *Frederick Law Olmsted, a Critic of the Old South*. *Stud Hist Pol Sci* (Hop), XLII. Baltimore, 1924.

19 GATELL, Frank Otto. *John Gorham Palfrey and the New England Conscience*. Cambridge, Mass., 1963.

20 KIBLER, Lillian A. *Benjamin F. Perry, South Carolina Unionist*. Durham, N.C., 1946.

21 BARTLETT, Irving H. *Wendell Phillips, Brahmin Radical*. Boston, 1961.

22 KORNGOLD, Ralph. *Two Friends of Man*. See 98.23.

23 SHERWIN, Oscar. *Prophet of Liberty: The Life and Times of Wendell Phillips*. New York, 1958.

24 NICHOLS, Roy F. *Franklin Pierce: Young Hickory of the Granite Hills*. Philadelphia, 1931.

25 DURDEN, Robert Franklin. *James Shepherd Pike: Republicanism and the American Negro, 1850–1882*. Durham, N.C., 1957.

D. Ray to Yancey

1 MONAGHAN, Jay. *The Man Who Elected Lincoln.* Indianapolis, 1956. (Charles H. Ray of the Chicago *Tribune*.)

2 WHITE, Laura A. *Robert Barnwell Rhett, Father of Secession.* New York, 1931.

3 AMBLER, Charles H. *Thomas Ritchie: A Study in Virginia Politics.* Richmond, 1913.

4 CRAVEN, Avery. *Edmund Ruffin, Southerner: A Study in Secession.* New York, 1932.†

5 SANBORN, F. B. *Recollections of Seventy Years.* 2 vols. Boston, 1909.

6 SCHAFER, Joseph. *Carl Schurz, Militant Liberal.* Evansville, Wis., 1930.

7 SCHURZ, Carl. *Reminiscences.* 3 vols. New York, 1907–1908.

8 BANCROFT, Frederic. *The Life of William H. Seward.* 2 vols. New York, 1900.

9 SHARROW, Walter G. "William Henry Seward: A Study in Nineteenth Century Politics and Nationalism, 1855–1861." Doctoral dissertation, University of Rochester, 1965.

10 VAN DEUSEN, Glyndon G. *William Henry Seward.* New York, 1967.

11 SHERMAN, John. *Recollections of Forty Years in the House, Senate and Cabinet.* 2 vols. Chicago, 1895.

12 SEARS, Louis M. *John Slidell.* Durham, N.C., 1925.

13 HARLOW, Ralph Volney. *Gerrit Smith, Philanthropist and Reformer.* New York, 1939.

14 THOMAS, Benjamin P., and Harold M. HYMAN. *Stanton: The Life and Times of Lincoln's Secretary of War.* New York, 1962.

15 VON ABELE, Rudolph. *Alexander H. Stephens: A Biography.* New York, 1946.

16 BRODIE, Fawn M. *Thaddeus Stevens, Scourge of the South.* New York, 1959.

17 CURRENT, Richard N. *Old Thad Stevens: A Story of Ambition.* Madison, Wis., 1942.

18 DONALD, David. *Charles Sumner and the Coming of the Civil War.* New York, 1960.

19 GOODMAN, Paul. "David Donald's *Charles Sumner* Reconsidered." *N Eng Q*, XXXVII(1964):373–387.

20 PIERCE, Edward. *Memoir and Letters of Charles Sumner.* 4 vols. Boston, 1877–1893. (Particularly, Vols. II and III.)

21 WYATT-BROWN, Bertrand. *Lewis Tappan and the Evangelical War against Slavery.* Cleveland, 1969.

22 DYER, Brainerd. *Zachary Taylor.* See 25.10.

23 HAMILTON, Holman. *Zachary Taylor, Soldier in the White House.* Indianapolis, 1951.

1 PHILLIPS, Ulrich Bonnell. *The Life of Robert Toombs*. New York, 1913.

2 THOMPSON, William Y. *Robert Toombs of Georgia*. Baton Rouge, 1966.

3 KRUG, Mark M. *Lyman Trumbull, Conservative Radical*. New York, 1965.

4 WHITE, Horace. *The Life of Lyman Trumbull*. Boston, 1913.

5 TREFOUSSE, Hans L. *Benjamin Franklin Wade, Radical Republican from Ohio*. New York, 1963.

6 VAN DEUSEN, Glyndon G. *Thurlow Weed, Wizard of the Lobby*. Boston, 1947.

7 WEST, Richard S., Jr. *Gideon Welles, Lincoln's Navy Department*. Indianapolis, 1943.

8 GOING, Charles B. *David Wilmot, Free-Soiler*. New York, 1924.

9 EATON, Clement. "Henry A. Wise, a Liberal of the Old South." *J S Hist*, VII(1941):482–494.

10 ZUBER, Richard L. *Jonathan Worth: A Biography of a Southern Unionist*. Chapel Hill, N.C., 1965.

11 DU BOSE, John W. *The Life and Times of William Lowndes Yancey*. Birmingham, Ala., 1892.

NOTES

INDEX

INDEX

INDEX

INDEX

INDEX

INDEX

INDEX

INDEX

INDEX

INDEX

INDEX

INDEX